Love *in* Action

Love *in* Action

Loving God and Neighbor:
A Twofold Commandment

Fernando Ocáriz

Scepter

This is a translation of Fernando Ocáriz, Amar con obras: A Dios y a los hombres, copyright © 2015, Ediciones Palabra, S.A., Madrid, Spain.

English translation, copyright © 2017 Scepter Publishers, Inc. New York with permission.

Scripture quotations are taken from the Revised Standard Version of the Bible: Second Catholic Edition, copyright © 1965, 1966, 2006 by the Division of Christian Education of the National Council of the Churches of Christ in the United States of America. Used by permission. All rights reserved. The Revised Standard Version of the Bible: Second Catholic Edition was published in 2006 with ecclesiastical approval of the United States Conference of Catholic Bishops.

Published by Scepter Publishers, Inc.
info@scepterpublishers.org
www.scepterpublishers.org
800-322-8773
New York

Translated by Christopher Schmitt
Text and cover design by Carol S. Cates

ISBN paperback 978-1-59417-291-5
ebook   978-1-59417-292-2

Library of Congress Cataloging-in-Publication Data

Names: Ocáriz Braña, Fernando, author.
Title: Love in action : loving God and neighbor : a twofold commandment / Fernando Ocáriz.
Other titles: Amar con obras. English
Description: New York : Scepter Publishers, 2017.
Identifiers: LCCN 2017013765 (print) | LCCN 2017015233 (ebook) | ISBN 9781594172922 (ebook) | ISBN 9781594172915 (pbk.)
Subjects: LCSH: God (Christianity)—Worship and love. | Love—Religious aspects—Christianity.
Classification: LCC BV4817 (ebook) | LCC BV4817 .O2313 2017 (print) | DDC 241/.4—dc23
LC record available at https://lccn.loc.gov/2017013765

Table of Contents

Part II

LOVING GOD

Part III

LOVING OUR NEIGHBOR AND THE WORLD

By Way of Introduction[1]

Parts of this book were published for the first time several decades ago. They are now offered in an updated and expanded form. The result is practically a new book. Like the first work, it is not meant to be a treatise on charity, but rather a collection of reflections, with no attempt to be exhaustive, about love for God and for our fellow men and women.

With a minimum of theological structure and distinctions, this great theme is considered here in some of its main aspects, with particular reference to the relationship between these two loves—love for God and love for others—that comprise one and the same charity. A correct grasp of this unity greatly facilitates understanding how and why charity is the core of Christian life, which is the life of God's children in Christ through the grace of the Holy Spirit, uncreated Love.

My intention here is to contribute to this understanding of charity's central role, while striving to listen to God in Holy Scripture. We will do so guided especially

[1] This is a translation of the author's introduction to the 2015 Spanish edition of the book.

by the Church's Magisterium, the teachings of St. Josemaría Escrivá de Balaguer, and, for certain topics, the teachings of the Fathers of the Church and St. Thomas Aquinas.

Fernando Ocáriz

Part I

The Twofold Precept
of Charity

> *"You shall love the Lord your God with all your heart, and with all your soul, and with all your mind. This is the great and first commandment. And a second is like it, You shall love your neighbor as yourself"*
> *(Mt 22:37–39).*

To help focus our reflections on this crucial twofold precept, we can cite at the beginning this long and splendid text of Benedict XVI:

Can we love God without seeing him? And can love be commanded? Against the double commandment of love these questions raise a double objection. No one has ever seen God, so how could we love him? Moreover, love cannot be commanded; it is ultimately a feeling that is either there or not, nor can it be produced by the will. Scripture seems to reinforce the first objection when it states, "If anyone says, 'I love God,' and hates his brother, he is a liar; for he who does not love his brother whom he has seen, cannot love God whom he has not seen" (1 Jn 4:20). But this text hardly excludes the love of God as something impossible. On the contrary, the whole context of the passage quoted from the First Letter of John shows that such love of God and love of neighbor is emphasized. One is so closely connected to the other that to say that we love God becomes a lie if we are closed to our neighbor or hate him altogether. St. John's words should rather be interpreted to mean that love of neighbor is a path that leads to the encounter with God and that closing our eyes to our neighbor also blinds us to God.

True, no one has ever seen God as he is. And yet God is not totally invisible to us: he does not remain completely inaccessible. God loved us first, says the Letter of John quoted above (see 4:10), and this love of God has appeared in our midst. He has become visible inasmuch as he "has sent his only Son into the world, so that we might live through him" (1 Jn 4:9). God has made himself visible: in Jesus we are able to see the Father (see Jn 14:9). Indeed, God is visible in a number of ways. In the love story recounted by the Bible, he comes toward us, he seeks to win our hearts, all the way to the Last Supper, to the piercing of his heart on the Cross, to his appearances after the Resurrection, and to the great deeds by which, through the activity of the Apostles, he guided the nascent Church along its path. Nor has the Lord been absent from subsequent Church history: he encounters us ever anew in the men and women who reflect his presence, in his Word, in the sacraments, and especially in the Eucharist. In the Church's Liturgy, in her prayer, in the living community of believers, we experience the love of God, we perceive his presence and we thus learn to recognize that presence in our daily lives. He has loved us first and he continues to do so; we too, then, can respond with love. God does not demand of us a feeling which we ourselves are incapable of producing. He loves us, he makes us see and experience his love, and since he has "loved us first," love can also blossom as a response within us.[2]

[2] Pope Benedict XVI, Encyclical on Christian Love *Deus caritas est* (December 25, 2005), nos. 16–17. As of February 2017, available at http://w2.vatican.va/content/benedict-xvi/en/encyclicals/documents/hf_ben-xvi_enc_20051225_deus-caritas-est.html.

Chapter 1

God's Love for Mankind

> In many and various ways God spoke of old to our fathers by the prophets; but in these last days he has spoken to us by a Son, whom he appointed the heir of all things, through whom also he created the ages. He reflects the glory of God and bears the very stamp of his nature, upholding the universe by his word of power. When he had made purification for sins, he sat down at the right hand of the Majesty on high. (Heb 1:1–3)

With these words inspired by God, the Letter to the Hebrews summarizes in a striking way many centuries of human history—a history that continuously shows forth God's merciful love for mankind and also the rebellions against God that have marred it. It is not a fictitious history but a true one made up of our free decisions, since from the beginning God wanted to "run the risk of our freedom."[1]

---

[1] St. Josemaría Escrivá, *Christ Is Passing By*, no. 113. As of February 2017, available at http://www.escrivaworks.org/book/christ_is_passing_by.htm.

God is the fullness of reality, infinite perfection.

Among the many ways, God has manifested himself to us in a special way, we can recall here the dialogue on Mont Horeb recounted in Exodus. God speaks to Moses from the burning bush: "I am the God of your father, the God of Abraham, the God of Isaac, and the God of Jacob" (Ex 3:6). Completely overwhelmed, Moses hides his face, not daring to look at God's majesty. And when he asks God for his name, he hears this answer: "'I AM WHO I AM.' And he said, 'Say this to the people of Israel, "I AM has sent me to you"'" (Ex 3:14).

This name for God ("He who is" or "Yahweh" in Hebrew) marks an important step in the progress of divine revelation. God speaks of himself in terms containing a great wealth of content, which the Fathers of the Church interpreted as referring to God in an absolute way, as he is in himself. Commenting on this passage, St. Jerome writes: "The Lord says in Exodus: *I am who I am.* And also: *Thus you will say to the children of Israel: He who is sent me to you.* So then only God existed, and the others didn't exist? The others receive their being from God as a gift. But God, who always is, does not have a beginning in any other. He himself is the origin and cause of his own substance."[2] And St. Augustine says: "God replied

---

[2] St. Jerome, *In Epistolas Paulinas ad Ephesios*, bk. 2, c. 3, 14: PL 26, 488.

that his name is Being. . . . For He exists in such a way that, compared to Him, creatures do not exist. But not compared to Him, creatures do exist insofar as they only exist because of Him. Compared with Him, they do not exist, because true Being is unchanging Being, which He alone is."[3]

Everything depends totally on God in its being and activity

God is the one who totally *Is*. He is not *this* thing or the *other*, but the fullness of being, the fullness of reality. Everything else, spiritual beings and bodily creatures, is or exists, but is not Being. Rather it *has* being, it has been made to be. God alone is the Absolute, without any condition. Everything else, including man, receives its being from God and therefore, is totally dependent, in its being and activity, on the Creator. Between the creature and the Creator there is an infinite, qualitative difference; between the infinite fullness of God and the infinite neediness of what is nothing, there is a gap that can be overcome only by the all-powerful and free action of God, ever present and grounding the very reality of everything that exists.

Mankind is situated within this created totality that we call the universe. Nevertheless, the likeness that every

[3] St. Augustine, *Enarrationes in Psalmos*, 134, 4: PL 37, 1741.

effect bears to its cause is very special in the case of man. God says, "Let us make man in our image, after our own likeness" (Gn 1:26). The human being is spiritual. We are intelligent and free, capable of determining ourselves, in a certain sense, by our knowledge of all that exists, and capable of making free decisions: freely accepting our ultimate end (God) or rejecting it. This freedom is expressed not only in making particular choices, but also and above all (on the more radical plane of personal being) in the capacity to decide on our ultimate destiny: "Often one hears people insisting unilaterally on freedom as our capacity to choose the means, while leaving aside the truth that freedom, in first place, is the power to decide on an end, and especially the end in its proper sense, which is the ultimate end."[4]

But this in no way diminishes our dependence on God. For we are sustained in our being and acting by a divine presence so intense that God is more intimate to each of us than we are to ourselves. As St. Augustine experienced in his own life, God is "*intimior intimo meo,*" more inward to me than my inmost self.[5]

---

[4] Translated from Luis Clavell, *Meatafysica e libertá,* (Roma: Armando, 1996), p. 184.

[5] St. Augustine, *Confessions,* III, 6, 11: PL 32, 688.

Divine presence, a presence of Love

In the face of this divine presence, we could at times feel afraid on seeing ourselves so intimately conditioned or dominated, and try to escape from this dominion. One of the psalms beautifully expresses God's inescapable presence:

> Where shall I go from your Spirit? Or where shall I flee from your presence? If I ascend to heaven, you are there! If I make my bed in Sheol, you are there! If I take the wings of the morning and dwell in the uttermost parts of the sea, even there your hand shall lead me, and your right hand shall hold me. If I say, "Let only darkness cover me, and the light about me be night," even the darkness is not dark to you, the night is bright as the day; for darkness is as light with you. (Ps 139:7–12)

Nevertheless, this divine presence is not an anonymous or indifferent one; it is a *presence of love.* God is Being, and as he himself has taught us, his Being is Love: *Deus caritas est* (1 Jn 4:8). This love is seen in the creation and holding in being of creatures. "God's love is the fundamental moving force in all created things: 'For you love all things that exist, and detest none of the things that you have made; for you would not have made anything if you had hated it' (Wis 11:24). Every creature is thus the object of the Father's tenderness."[6]

With the human being, God's love is also seen in the elevation of the created spirit to the supernatural order and in the glory God has prepared for us. God's presence of love in the soul in grace is most intense, and awakens in the soul a personal response. As St. Josemaría said: "We will strive to be aware of God's presence, just as people in love are always thinking about each other."[7] And Benedict XVI insisted, "God's love for us is fundamental for our lives, and it raises important questions about who God is and who we are."[8]

At the beginning of human history, sin entered the world

But human freedom, limited and fallible as it is, could and, in fact, did rebel against God's plans. At the very dawn of history, sin irrupted in the world: a sin of rebellion, an attempt to replace God with man. "You will be like God" (Gn 3:5), the devil deceptively promised. And just as God had granted our first parents the gift of

[6] Pope Francis, Encyclical on Care for Our Common Good *Laudato sí* (May 24, 2015), no. 77. As of February 2017, available at http://w2.vatican.va/content/dam/francesco/pdf/encyclicals/documents/papa-francesco_20150524_enciclica-laudato-si_en.pdf.

[7] St. Josemaría, *Christ Is Passing By*, no. 119. Prayer itself becomes a response to this continual presence of love: see G. Derville, entry for *Oración*, in J. L. Illanes (coordinator), *Diccionario de San Josemaría Escrivá de Balaguer* (Monte Carmelo: Burgos 2013), pp. 903–904.

[8] Benedict XVI, *Deus caritas est*, no. 2.

grace and justice to transmit it to all mankind, so sin was likewise transmitted to all men and women from then on by generation.

Divine love, however, did not abandon mankind to the destiny our first parents had chosen: a destiny of separation from the true and infinite Good, a destiny of misery and condemnation. Rather, after Adam and Eve's sin, God once again seeks us out. His judgment of the first sin is immediately followed by his promise of redemption (see Gn 3:14–15). Throughout Israel's history, he was preparing for this redemption: the Covenant, the Law, the Prophets. . . . These centuries are marked by God's love for mankind seen in the history of salvation, where God's faithfulness shines out despite the infidelity of men and women. In his constant, loving calls, mankind finds not only justice but also mercy and pardon, as Yahweh was preparing the path that will lead to our salvation. This is the meaning of Divine Law, another manifestation of God's love that marks out the boundaries beyond which the path disappears, only to become a precipice.

To accept this reality, we need to acknowledge that God has made us free so that, always and in everything, we might freely do what is good for the sake of love. The sobering possibility of choosing evil "is not freedom or any part of it, though it is a sign of freedom,"[9] just as

---

[9] St. Thomas Aquinas, *De veritate*, q. 22, a. 6c.

error, properly speaking, is not knowledge or even part of knowledge, although it is a sign of having an intellect. The possibility of choosing evil, the possibility of sinning, is a consequence of our limitation as a creature.

"Can a woman forget her sucking child, that she should have no compassion on the son of her womb? Even these may forget, yet I will not forget you" (Is 49:15). When we come to realize the immensity of God's love, and listen to his promise to be faithful; when we contemplate God's infinite self-sufficiency, his infinite fullness of Being, and contrast it with our own infinite neediness and nothingness, the only fitting response is grateful adoration and deep admiration: "What is man that you are mindful of him, and the son of man that you care for him?" (Ps 8:4).

The fullness of time: Christ

God's love knows no limits. "When the time had fully come, God sent forth his Son, born of woman, born under the law, to redeem those who were under the law, so that we might receive adoption as sons. And because you are sons, God has sent the Spirit of his Son into our hearts, crying, 'Abba! Father!' So through God you are no longer a slave but a son, and if a son then an heir" (Gal 4:4–7).

For the person who lives by faith, history is not fundamentally an indefinite and tentative advance toward a future where the complete happiness we all yearn for is always yet further in the future. Nor is it a cyclic succession of phenomena which is not affected by our decisions.

> If we take a look at the course of human history, we will see progress and advances. Science has made man more aware of his power. Technology today controls the world much more than in the past, helping men to reach their dream of a greater level of culture, unity and material well being.
>
> Some people are perhaps inclined to tone down this optimism, reminding us that men still suffer from injustice and wars, at times worse than those of the past. They may well be right. But, above and beyond these considerations, I prefer to remember that in the religious sphere man is still man and God is still God. In this sphere the peak of progress has already been reached. And that peak is Christ, alpha and omega, the beginning of all things and their end (see Rv 21:6).
>
> In the spiritual life, there is no new era to come. Everything is already there, in Christ who died and rose again, who lives and stays with us always.[10]

In Christ, God's love for us has been made manifest in a

---

[10] St. Josemaría, *Christ Is Passing By*, no. 104.

moving way: in his birth, in how he treated those who followed or encountered him, in his entire life, and above all, in his Passion and death on the cross, in his glorious Resurrection and in his self-giving in the Holy Eucharist. "In this is love, not that we loved God but that he loved us and sent his Son to be the expiation for our sins" (1 Jn 4:10). And as St. John Paul II says, our Lord's love is especially seen in its fullness when we direct our eyes and heart to the Blessed Eucharist: "The gaze of the Church is constantly turned to the Lord present in the Sacrament of the Altar, in which she discovers the full manifestation of his boundless love."[11]

God's love, mercy, and justice

"I will rejoice and be glad for your merciful love, because you have seen my lowliness, you have taken heed of my adversities" (Ps 31:7). The Old Testament frequently invites us, especially in the Psalms, to joyfully praise and thank God for his mercy in the face of human wretchedness. Divine love is poured out on our smallness and weakness as creatures, in order to forgive and raise us up. Above all in the New Testament, in Christ, divine mercy is revealed in its fullness:

[11] St. John Paul II, Encyclical on the Eucharist and Its Relationship to the Church *Ecclesia de Eucharistia* (April 17, 2003), no. 1. As of February 2017, available at http://www.vatican.va/holy_father/special_features/encyclicals/documents/hf_jp-ii_enc_20030417_ecclesia_eucharistia_en.html.

In Christ and through Christ, God also becomes especially visible in his mercy; that is to say, there is emphasized that attribute of the divinity which the Old Testament, using various concepts and terms, already defined as "mercy." Christ confers on the whole of the Old Testament tradition about God's mercy a definitive meaning. Not only does He speak of it and explain it by the use of comparisons and parables, but above all He Himself makes it incarnate and personifies it. He Himself, in a certain sense, is mercy. To the person who sees it in Him—and finds it in Him—God becomes "visible" in a particular way as the Father "who is rich in mercy" (Eph 2:4).[12]

Because of God's perfect simplicity, divine mercy is identical not only to his infinite love, but also to his justice. This reality, which our intellect can comprehend only in a very limited and analogous way, reveals its character as a mystery in a number of different ways. The most notable one is the so-called "permission of evil," and perhaps even more forcefully the existence of divine judgment and the possibility of condemnation. We should ponder the reality that "God is justice and

---

[12] St. John Paul II, Encyclical on the Mercy of *God Dives in misericordia* (November 30, 1980), no. 2. As of February 2017, available at http://w2.vatican.va/content/john-paul-ii/en/encyclicals/documents/hf_jp-ii_enc_30111980_dives-in-misericordia.html.

creates justice. This is our consolation and our hope. And in his justice, there is also grace. This we know by turning our gaze to the crucified and risen Christ. Both these things—justice and grace—must be seen in their correct inner relationship. Grace does not cancel out justice. It does not make wrong into right. It is not a sponge which wipes everything away, so that whatever someone has done on earth ends up being of equal value."[13]

In the face of evil in all its forms, including what is not directly attributable to the bad use of human freedom, Christians can and should maintain their faith in God's love and their hope by contemplating Jesus on the cross. It is above all on the cross that he reveals to us the identity between divine justice and mercy. In any case, before the mystery of God and his Providence, the proper attitude is always one of silent adoration: "*indicibilia deitatis casto silentio venerantes*—venerating what is ineffable in the divinity with a chaste silence."[14]

---

[13] Pope Benedict XVI, Encyclical on Christian Hope *Spe salvi* (November 30, 2007), no. 44. As of February 2017, available at http://w2.vatican.va/content/benedict-xvi/en/encyclicals/documents/hf_ben-xvi_enc_20071130_spe-salvi.html.

[14] Pseudo Dionysius, *De divinis nominibus*, ch. I, no. 11 (quoted in St. Thomas, *In librum Dionysii de Divinis Nominibus expositio*, para. 3, 11).

Chapter 2

Our Love for God

If we contemplate Christ Jesus, in whom "the whole deity dwells bodily" (Col 2:9), seeing that "having loved his own who were in the world, he loved them to the end" (Jn 13:1); if we consider carefully how, on the eve of his Passion, he gave himself for us with an ardent desire, as a sacrifice and as nourishment in the Holy Eucharist, then we will readily understand that the deepest meaning of each of our lives lies in loving God, giving him the glory that is his due: "If life didn't have as its aim to give glory to God, it would be detestable—even more, loathsome."[1]

To give glory to God, to love God, is not merely something important for us men and women, such as being grateful or responding to the love we have received. It is the only thing that matters absolutely, since it is the only true fulfilment of our human potential, without which our life is empty and meaningless: "All men who were ignorant of God were foolish by nature," the Book of

[1] St. Josemaría Escrivá, *The Way*, no. 783. As of February 2017, available at http://www.escrivaworks.org/book/the_way.htm.

Wisdom teaches. "And they were unable from the good things that are seen to know him who exists, nor did they recognize the craftsman while paying heed to his works" (Wis 13:1).

Love and law

Divine Law is a pathway, not a roadblock. God tells us in his Law that the first and greatest commandment is to love Him. "Hear, O Israel: the Lord our God is one Lord,' and you shall love the Lord your God with all your heart, and with all your soul, and with all your might" (Dt 6:4–5). Long afterwards, God himself became man in Christ: he was the light that shone in the darkness, but the darkness did not receive it (see Jn 1:5). Trying to tempt Christ, to twist his words, a Pharisee asked our Lord: "Which is the great commandment in the law?" Perhaps the man was hoping Christ would say something that would allow him to accuse him. But our Lord answered: "You shall love the Lord your God with all your heart, and with all your soul, and with all your mind. This is the great and first commandment" (Mt 22:37). After confirming the supreme precept with words from the Book of Deuteronomy, Jesus added, also with words from Holy Scripture (in Leviticus): "And the second is like it, You shall love your neighbor as yourself" (Mt 22:39).

"With all your heart": this is the rule and measure of the love that God asks of us. It is a love without measure, a total love. God does not ask just for a place in our heart, in our soul, in our mind, where we make space for him alongside our others loves. Rather he wants all our love: not just a little of our love or our life, a measure of it. God is the All, the Only One, the Absolute, and so should be loved *ex toto corde*, with all our heart, absolutely. He doesn't "need" our love or the glory we can give him: he is the fullness of Being, infinitely self-sufficient. He is the All, and we cannot add anything to him. But he wants the glory and love that we as creatures owe him, and to the extent that we achieve this we attain full happiness, union with God, which he himself has offered us with his gift of creation, elevation to the supernatural order, and redemption. God wants our happiness, which consists in leading a life in communion with him: "God's glory is man truly alive, and the life of man is the vision of God."[2]

Truly loving someone includes the desire, effective if possible, to obtain that person's good. This is called benevolence. But love is not only benevolence; it is also the desire for the presence of the beloved and union.[3]

---

[2] St. Irenaeus, *Adversus haereses*, IV, 20, 7: PG 7, 1037.
[3] Joseph Pieper has a valuable discussion of the various philosophical conceptions of love in *Faith, Hope, Love*, Ignatius Press, 1986.

Moreover, we can desire and procure someone's good without loving that person, as when we carry out a service for someone without taking any real interest in that person.

At the same time, we should realize that it is impossible for us to have "an absolutely pure love" for God, one that excludes any desire for our own good, since love is not only benevolence.[4] As St. Thomas said, "If God were not a true good for man (which is an impossible assumption), there would be no reason for man to love at all."[5]

But if true love includes benevolence, what good can we give God that God does not already have? In other words, what do our acts of worship, adoration, or observance of his commandments give to God? Using the language of analogy—similarity within a greater dissimilarity—that necessarily characterizes our knowledge of God, can we think of God as "lacking" something if we fail to give Him our love, our union with Him, which is precisely our happiness? Here again we are reminded of the "risk" God wanted to take in creating us free. At the same time we must reaffirm the truth, an apparent paradox, that God doesn't need us at all, for he alone is "capable of loving without being dependent on being

---

[4] On the union of these two dimensions of love, usually called eros and agape, in their original meanings, see Benedict XVI, *Deus caritas est*, especially nos. 6–7.

[5] St. Thomas Aquinas, *Summa Theologiae*, II-II, q. 26, a. 13 ad 3.

loved in return; it is a divine privilege always to be less the beloved than the lover."[6] Nevertheless, God has chosen to "need" us: "Each of us is the result of a thought of God. Each of us is willed, each of us is loved, each of us is necessary."[7]

Loving God, neighbor, and oneself

God is All, but all is not God. And the One who asks us for *all* our love, also asks us, somewhat surprisingly, to love others, and assumes that we already love ourselves: "You shall love your neighbor as yourself" (Mt 22:39). A certain unity seems to exist between God, neighbor, and oneself, insofar as all three can and should be loved. An equality between oneself and other men and women is established, which in a certain sense extends to all created beings. Love for oneself, self-love, understood in its original and necessary form, is the desire for happiness.[8]

God is to be loved not as one among others, nor even more than others, as though he were the first in a series. Rather he is to be loved in a different way: absolutely, without measure, without any intrinsic reference to any

[6] Joseph Pieper, *Faith, Hope, Love* (San Francisco: Ignatius Press, 1986), p. 184.

[7] Benedict XVI, *Homily*, April 24, 2005. As of February 2017, available at http://w2.vatican.va/content/benedict-xvi/en/homilies/2005/documents/hf_ben-xvi_hom_20050424_inizio-pontificato.html.

[8] See St. Augustine, *Sermon* 368: PL 39, 1655.

other being. Although he is the fullness of Being, God is not the being of things; each created being, including the human being, has its own consistency: it is, or exists, in itself, and thus can be known and loved. Hence, we do not love God simply by loving our neighbor, even though not loving our neighbor is a sign of not loving God, since if we love God we will also love all that he has made and loves. The quality of our love, moreover, determines the quality of the person we are. "Love, as the primal act of the will, is simultaneously the point of origin and center of existence as a whole. What kind of person one is will be decided at this point."[9]

The proper attitude of a spiritual creature before the Creator is adoration, the total submission of our will. This is the only attitude that adequately corresponds to our real situation before God. In the words of Pope Francis: "Worshipping the Lord means giving him the place that he must have; worshipping the Lord means stating, believing—not only by our words—that he alone truly guides our lives; worshipping the Lord means that we are convinced before him that he is the only God, the God of our lives, the God of our history."[10]

---

[9] Pieper, *Faith, Hope, Love*, p. 167.

[10] Pope Francis, *Homily in St. Paul Outside-the-Walls*, April 14, 2013, no. 3. As of February 2017, available at http://w2.vatican.va/content/francesco/en/homilies/2013/documents/papa-francesco_20130414_omelia-basilica-san-paolo.html.

Furthermore, God himself has gratuitously made us his children and sharers in his divine nature. The filiation within the Godhead is unique and subsistent: it is the natural filiation of the Word, who is the Person of the Son. But in his infinite mercy and love, God has deigned to raise us up to participate in this filiation, to be truly God's sons and daughters: "See what love the Father has given us, that we should be called children of God: and so we are" (1 Jn 3:1). The Word continues being the *Only-Begotten*, the Only Son, but we participate in this unique filiation, without thereby multiplying or diminishing it. We are sons of God *in* the Son through the sanctifying power of the Holy Spirit.[11]

Divine filiation is *identification with Christ*. It is not merely being like God, having his sentiments, reactions, viewpoint on reality, etc., although it includes all of this. Rather it is to be part of the same and unique relationship that Christ, the Incarnate Word, enjoys with God the Father. We are children of God, not on our own, but only through being one in Christ. We are God's children because we participate—and therefore in a partial and limited way—in his filiation: through him, with him, and in him we make up one sole body, his Mystical Body. St. Josemaría said very forcefully that, thanks to

---

[11] See St. Augustine, *Contra Faustum*, bk. 3, c. 3: PL 42, 2152; St. Cyril of Alexandria, De adoratione in Spiritu, bk. 1: PG 68, 146–147.

supernatural grace, a Christian is not only *alter Christus,* another Christ, but *ipse Christus,* Christ himself.[12]

God in us and we in God

On being raised to the supernatural order, God's presence in the very core of our being, takes on a new dimension. God is in us because he created us; but when *we are raised to the supernatural plane of existence,* we are in God: "God is love, and he who abides in love abides in God, and God abides in him" (1 Jn 4:16). These words from the First Letter of John express with remarkable clarity the heart of our faith: the Christian image of God, and the resulting image of our own being and destiny. In the same verse St. John also offers us, as it were, a summary of Christian life: "We have come to know and to believe in the love God has for us."[13]

We are invited to share in God's intimate life. From having been strangers, we have now become members of God's family (see Eph 2:19). Our love for God is no longer the product of a finite will, but the charity that he himself pours into our hearts (see Rom 5:5), as a certain sharing in personal and subsistent Love: the Holy Spirit.[14] And this love, this charity necessarily

---

[12] See Fernando Ocariz, *God, the Church and the World: An Interview with the Auxiliary Vicar of Opus Dei* (Downers Grove, IL: Midwest Theological Forum, 2015), p. 10.

[13] See Benedict XVI, *Deus caritas est,* no. 1.

[14] See St. Thomas, *Summa Theologiae,* II-II, q. 24, a. 7c.

reaches out in a new love for others, which leads to a different and deeper union among all men and women—a union that is not horizontal, but convergence in Christ. St. Josemaría, who had a special awareness of our divine filiation and of the resultant fraternity among all men and women, gave eloquent expression to this union:

Our Lord has come to bring peace, good news and life to all men. Not only to the rich, not only to the poor. Not only to the wise nor only to the simple. To everyone, to the brothers, for brothers we are, children of the same Father, God. So there is only one race, the race of the children of God. There is only one color, the color of the children of God. And there is only one language: the language which speaks to the heart and to the mind, without the noise of words, making us know God and love one another.[15]

[15] St. Josemaría, *Christ Is Passing By*, no. 106.

Chapter 3

Risk of Adulterating Christianity

Christian life requires constant spiritual progress in fidelity to the Gospel and in service to all souls. To respond to this requirement, we need to struggle against our tendency to become spiritually "bourgeois" and strive to faithfully transmit Christ's message to others, being ready, like St. Paul, to become all things to all men, and so save all (see 1 Cor 9:22). And we should do so being ever mindful that it is not our own strength that saves souls but God's grace.

Confronting modernity and post-modernity

A renewed concern has arisen in our own day and age to preach the Gospel in a manner that is acceptable to so-called "modern man" and now "postmodern man." These expressions, rather vague and hard to define, can be understood in a variety of ways according to the respective philosophical and ideological presuppositions on which they are based. In any case, to preach the Gospel in a manner that is suitable to its hearers has always been and will always be a requirement of evangelization. Nevertheless, at the root of some of the attempts to adapt the Christian message to modern and postmodern ears we find the concept of a world now "come of age," an "adult" world that requires the preaching of an "adult" Christianity dispensing with traditional approaches and outlooks that are viewed as unacceptable in the contemporary cultural context.

This "coming of age" is seen as requiring, among other things, the awareness of mankind's autonomy and power over the world. Hence, with differing premises, the need is postulated in some sectors to "liberate" the Gospel message from anything that is no longer intelligible or believable for the secularized, pragmatic, and scientific mentality of our times.

In the most extreme cases, the misguided desire to present the Gospel in a form acceptable to today's world is based on a clear anti-supernatural *a priori*: Anything is seen as problematical to the extent that it requires the supernatural. But the real underlying problem is our human resistance to whatever surpasses us.

If we examine one by one the grave problems afflicting theology today, we always find the same underlying prejudice: the Church is a problem if it claims to be divine; Christ is a problem if he claims to be the Son of God; Sacred Scripture is a problem if it claims to be inspired; morality is a problem if it claims to be divine law and not a human creation

. . . . The truly great problem is only one: God.[1]

Presenting religion in a manner acceptable to modern man seems to mean, in some cases, disregarding God little by little and replacing him with man, even to the point of holding that the meaning of religion, in theory and practice, is service rendered to mankind. And as a result, any supernatural feature is sometimes obscured or even denied when presenting the Person and mission of Christ.

Utopia of a future earthly paradise

God and eternal life cannot be replaced by the utopia of progress towards a future earthly paradise, as recent history makes so dramatically clear. "In the modern world there is a tendency to reduce man to his horizontal dimension alone. But without an openness to the Absolute, what does man become? The answer to this question is found in the experience of every individual, but it is also written in the history of humanity with the blood shed in the name of ideologies or by political regimes which have sought to build a 'new humanity' without God."[2]

[1] Translated from Carlos Cardona, *Metafísica de la opción intelectual* (Madrid: Rialp, 1969), p. 115.

[2] St. John Paul II, Encyclical on the Permanent Validity of the Church's Missionary Mandate *Redemptoris missio* (December 7, 1990), no. 8. As of February 2017, available at http://w2.vatican.va/content/john-paul-ii/en/encyclicals/documents/hf_jp-ii_enc_07121990_redemptoris-missio.html.

Divine transcendence cannot be replaced by the "transcendence" of man in history: an indefinite process of human, earthly perfection, without beginning or end, and without any objective and stable standard of judgment. God then turns out to be the human error of having personalized this tendency towards the future. In that case, only time-bound and utopian religions would be possible. It would be meaningless to speak about God, since God would be nothing but man himself, and man would be identified with God (God who acts through love and self-giving). The Incarnation of the Word would be nothing but the mythical expression of this Incarnation of the Eternal in history, of the Absolute in the conditioned, of the Infinite in the finite, of the Transcendent in the here and now. This is the only meaning that Bultmann, in his attempt to "demythologize" the Gospel, could find in St. John's prologue: "*Et Verbum caro factum est, et habitavit in nobis*—the Word became flesh and dwelt among us."

The "death of God" and the worship of man

If the sense of God's transcendence is lost, besides forgetting our real situation before God, we run the risk, both old and new, of falling into historicism, which sees history as the very core of reality, as the privileged and even exclusive place of truth. In that case, the present annuls the past, and is negated in turn by a future that is just as fleeting and ephemeral as the present it negates. This path leads in the end to speaking about the "death of God" and to formulating contradictory "theologies of the death of God." Using a language that is Christian only in appearance, at times only paganism and apostasy remain.

These currents of thought are not easy to analyze. Their development reflects a complex process with deep roots, whose analysis would require talking about liberal Protestantism and modernism, and their common origins.[3]

It is surprising to see how relevant today is the voice, raised from within Protestantism, of Kierkegaard, a deeply religious person, in his lively polemic with Hegel's system:

> The fundamental confusion, the original sin, of Christendom is that year after year, decade after decade, century after century, it has pursued the insidious purpose—just about half conscious of what it would, and essentially unconscious of what it did—of tricking God out of his rights as the proprietor of Christianity, and has got it into its head that the race, the human race, was itself the inventor, or

---

[3] For a philosophical and theological treatment of this topic, see Carlos Cardona, *Metafísica de la opción intellectual* and R. García de Haro, *Historia teológica de Modernismo* (Pamplona: Eunsa, , 1972).

had come pretty close to inventing Christianity. Just
as in civil law a fortune reverts to the state when it
has lain unclaimed for a certain period of years and
no heir presents himself—so has the race, pervert-
ed by observation of the trivial fact that Christianity
is a thing that actually exists, thought within itself as
follows: "It is now so long a time since God has let
Himself be heard from as proprietor and master
that Christianity has consequently reverted to us,
who can either decide to abolish it altogether, or to
modify it *ad libitum*, very much as we might deal with
our own possession or invention, treating Christianity, not as something which *in obedient subservience to
God's majesty* MUST be believed, but as something
which in order to be acceptable must try by the aid
of *reasons* to satisfy 'the age,' 'the public,' 'this dis-
tinguished assembly,' etc."

Every revolt in science . . . against moral disci-
pline, every revolt in social life . . . against obedience, every revolt in political life . . . against worldly rule, is connected with and derived from this
revolt against God with respect to Christianity. This
revolt—the abuse of the "human race"' as a catego-
ry—does not, however, resemble the revolt of the
Titans, for it is in the sphere of *reflection*, insidiously
carried out from year to year, from generation to
generation. Reflection constantly takes only a tiny

little bit at a time, and about this little bit one can constantly say, "Why, in small matters one may well yield"—until in the end reflection will have taken everything without anybody noticing it, because it came about little by little. . . .

All doubt (which, be it observed parenthetically, is just simply disobedience to God—when it is ethically considered and not made a fuss about with an air of scientific superiority)—all doubt has ultimately its stronghold in the illusion of temporal existence that we are a lot of us, pretty much the whole of humanity, which in the end can jolly well overawe God and be itself the Christ. And pantheism is an acoustic illusion which confounds *vox populi* with *vox dei*, an optical illusion, a cloud-picture formed out of the mists of temporal existence, a mirage formed by reflection from temporal existence and regarded as the eternal.[4]

This progressive substitution of God by man reaches its culmination, at least in theory, with Hegel, who asserted that the essence of God, if it were not the essence of man and nature, would be absolutely nothing. From there it was a short step to Feuerbach's doing away completely with the very idea of God, which Hegel had held

---

[4] Soren Kierkegaard, *The Point of View for My Work as an Author* (New York: Harper Torchbook, 1962), pp. 132–135.

onto only out of a vague "Christian nostalgia." And thereby the way was opened for the militant atheism of Marx's dialectical and historical materialism.[5]

When we turn to the influence these ideas have had on human history, it is evident how over time the same atheistic ideologies that championed the exaltation of man and the "death of God" have led to the attempt to exterminate humanity. The twentieth century witnessed the cruel spectacle of the Marxist and Nazi totalitarian states that have facilely justified the elimination of millions of human beings on the altar of a supposed blessing for the collectivity, along with the violation of fundamental human rights and widespread impoverishment. More recently, within "transhumanist" currents of thought, the goal is to raise human capacities to new heights by altering our genetic structure. A freedom totally emancipated from nature is aspired to, which in the end can lead only to the dissolution of the human person, reduced to a material object open to manipulation by others.

Although often unnoticed, the influence of philosophy on all levels of human society is greater than is sometimes thought. Likewise, the influence exerted by the prevailing mentality of a society in the genesis of a

[5] For a study of the origin of atheism in modern philosophy, see Cornelio Fabro, *God in Exile: Modern Atheism* (Charlotte, NC: Newman Press, 1968). See also Fernando Ocariz, *El Marzismo. Teoría y práctica de una revolución* (Madrid: Palabra, 1980), pp. 21–43.

new philosophy is also considerable. Nor should we forget that errors have always appeared on the scene mixed with a partial truth, for otherwise no one would accept them. So, it is important not to let ourselves be deceived by the apparently valid aspects of certain outlooks, when these are also inseparably linked with the denial of other fundamental truths. We see this in the apparent charity towards others, the apparent respect for human dignity contained in humanism or philanthropy, etc., which often masks the resistance to God, whether militant or agnostic, that underlies many false philosophies today, and that little by little seems to be seeping into some Christian environments.

True human greatness

Mankind has a great value, for we have been created in God's image and redeemed at a great price (see 1 Cor 6:20), the blood of Christ. But this doesn't make us the center of everything. We always need to keep a humble attitude before God's majesty, for it is only in relationship to God that we acquire our true greatness.

If a man is not humble, he will try to make God his own, but not in the divine way which Christ made possible when he said: "Take, eat; this is my body." The proud man tries to confine the grandeur of God within human limits. Then reason—the cold, blind one that is so different from the mind imbued with faith, and even from the well-directed mind of someone capable of enjoying and loving things— becomes irrational in its attempt to reduce everything to cramped human experience. The truth surpassing man's intelligence is thus impoverished, and a person's heart develops a crust rendering it insensitive to the action of the Holy Spirit. Our limited intelligence would be completely at a loss then if the merciful power of God did not break down the barriers of our wretchedness. "A new heart I will give you, and a new spirit I will put within you; and I will take out of your flesh your heart of stone and give you a heart of flesh." Only with God's help will the soul see again and be filled with joy on hearing the promises of sacred Scripture.[6]

A direct profession of atheism clearly makes no sense for anyone claiming to find support for their ideas in the Gospel. Nevertheless, we have witnessed the incoherence of a "Christian atheism" that seeks to uproot from the Gospel the "myth of the divine," so as to retain what is of value in the teaching of this "great man" who was Jesus of Nazareth. Thus, the true "secular meaning of the Gospel" would be brought to light and the "Gospel of Christian atheism" could finally be presented.

[6] St. Josemaría, *Christ Is Passing By*, no.165.

Even though such an approach is self-contradictory, as we just said, in some sectors of modern thought the attempt is made to dilute any relationship with God into human relationships.

The claim that God is nothing but man (however this statement is understood) violates both human reason and, above all, a Christian vision of the world. Nevertheless, the practical consequences of substituting man for God have infiltrated the mindset of some thinkers who view God as being "too distant" or "too transcendent." They have misinterpreted and twisted the meaning of St. John's words: "He who does not love his brother whom he has seen, cannot love God whom he has not seen" (1 Jn 4:20). And they even come to interpret "love for God" as meaning simply "love for neighbor." So, it is not surprising that they should go on to say, for example, that the sin of the world is to say *no* to man and the world, and that religion (now that God has become incarnate) is authentically Christian only insofar as it is service to mankind.

Christianity is not reducible to any humanism

The theoretical identification of man with God (which is theoretical atheism), and the concept of an indifferent and distant God lead in practice to the same conclusion: making man, individually and socially, the center of everything, as if he were absolute. It would be inter-

esting to make an historical analysis of the mutual influence of these two positions; apparently opposed to one
another, they both lead to the same practical result of
dispensing with God. Theoretical atheism does so from
the very start, as a basic postulate; in the second case,
this happens little by little, and even without realizing it.
The first approach, reducing God to man, is easily rejected by a Christian mindset; more insidious is the second approach that *in practice* also tends to do without
God by viewing love for our fellow men as the only work-
able meaning of Christianity.

In some cases these approaches, rather than resting
on a fundamental error, are the result of highlighting
especially one aspect (love for others), while taking for
granted the aspect of adoration and love for God. But in
other cases, often stemming from an unjustified inferi-
ority complex in confrontation with Marxist ideologies,
the intent was not simply to present *one part* of Christianity while being silent about the other; rather the aim
in the end was to carry out a deep *falsification* of the
Christian message. Here, it is not simply a case of dispensing money of little value, with only half the value
required. Rather it means dispensing false money, since
love for neighbor that is not united to love for God and
subordinated to that love (object of the first and most
important of the commandments) cannot buy entry to
heaven, either for oneself or others.

Truly enlightening are St. Paul's words written to the Corinthians about charity, without which giving all our goods to others, and even our very life, would be futile:

> If I speak in the tongues of men and of angels, but have not love, I am a noisy gong or a clanging cymbal. And if I have prophetic powers, and understand all mysteries and all knowledge, and if I have all faith, so as to remove mountains, but have not love, I am nothing. If I give away all I have, and if I deliver my body to be burned, but have not love, I gain nothing." (1 Cor 13:1–3)

Referring to these words, St. Josemaría remarks that "the charity described by St. Paul is not just philanthropy, humanitarianism, or an understandable sympathy for the sufferings of others. Rather it requires the practice of the theological virtue of loving God and of loving others for the sake of God."[7]

Of course, the danger also exists of interpreting Christianity in an individualistic manner, as if the only thing important were an apparent attitude of adoration or concern for doctrinal declarations, without lifting a finger to help others. Then prayer becomes superficial and doctrine loses life. Although theoretically affirming the central role of Christ, his image soon fades away.

---

[7] St. Josemaría Escrivá, *Friends of God*, no. 235. As of February 2017, available at http://www.escrivaworks.org/book/friends_of_god-point-235.htm

The Christian message is diluted, and its demands for a real and active charity are silenced. Dedication to our neighbor, we should never forget, stems from seeing in them Christ's face. As we will have occasion to consider later, the root and foundation of love for neighbor is love for God.

Chapter 4

The Newness of Christian Love

"*Madatum novum do vobis, ut diligatis invicem*—A new commandment I give to you, that you love one another" (Jn 13:34). This "newness" is not the substitution or the "translation" of "love for God" by "love for neighbor." Nor is Christ teaching us that love and faithfulness to God is simply love and faithfulness to mankind and our world.

The Gospel itself makes clear that the "newness" of Christian love with respect to the Old Testament does not lie in replacing love for God with love for neighbor. In the first place, the Old Testament too prescribed, along with love for God, love for our neighbor. Love for God, certainly, stood out as the fundamental commandment, oriented above all to worship and the fulfillment of the divine precepts: "Hear, O Israel: The Lord our God is one Lord; and you shall love the Lord your God with all your heart, and with all your soul, and with all your might" (Dt 6:4–5). Deuteronomy also teaches: "You shall therefore love the Lord your God, and keep his charge, his statutes, his ordinances, and his commandments always" (11:1). And divine Wisdom in the Book of Sirach tells us that we are to love God as our Creator: "With all your might love your Maker" (7:30).

But love for our fellow men and women is also repeatedly commanded in the Old Testament, as Christ himself reminds us by quoting the words from Leviticus: "You shall love your neighbor as yourself" (19:18). The Israelites were commanded to love not just other Israelites, but every human being. "When a stranger sojourns with you in your land, you shall not do him wrong. The stranger who sojourns with you shall be to you as the native among you, and you shall love him as yourself" (Lv 19:33–34).

Primacy of love for God over the inseparable love for neighbor

The primacy of love for God over love for neighbor is announced at times in Scripture with phrases that overwhelm us with their forcefulness: "If your brother, the son of your mother, or your son, or your daughter, or the wife of your bosom, or your friend who is as your own soul, entices you secretly, saying, 'Let us go and serve other gods' . . . [y]ou shall stone him to death with stones, because he sought to draw you away from the Lord your God" (Dt 13:6–11). Regardless of the historical circumstances behind this precept, imposed to keep the Israelites free from idolatry, this command contains

a perennial teaching: Our love for God must be absolute, not constrained even by the deepest and most no-
ble human love. Love for oneself and for our neighbor
can never be invested with this mark of absolute totality
but rather, must always be subordinated to love for God.

"A new commandment I give to you, that you love one
another; even as I have loved you, that you also love one
another" (Jn 13:34). The newness, then, is not in the
words "love one another," since this was already prescribed in the Old Law, but rather in "even as I have
loved you," which our Lord sets forth as the measure of
our love for others. Therefore, the innovation of Christian love can only be understood by first meditating on
how Christ loved us: "Now before the feast of the Pass-
over, when Jesus knew that his hour had come to depart
out of this world to the Father, having loved his own who
were in the world, he loved them to the end" (Jn 13:1).

The new commandment is not the "metamorphosis"
of "love for God" into "love for others." Jesus himself
frequently and unequivocally reaffirms the priority of
love for God over love for our fellow men and women:
"He who loves father or mother more than me is not
worthy of me; and he who loves son or daughter more
than me is not worthy of me" (Mt 10:37). St. Luke cites
another similar expression of Jesus that is even stron-
ger: "If any one comes to me and does not hate his own

father and mother and wife and children and brothers and sisters, yes, and even his own life, he cannot be my disciple" (Lk 14:26). Hence the Church condemned many centuries ago the assertion that "one who loves God more than neighbor certainly does well, but does not yet act perfectly."[1]

Sacred Scripture teaches clearly that the fundamental motive for loving our neighbor should be love for God, since this leads us to love what God loves, imitating God's love for all men and women. "You have heard that it was said, 'You shall love your neighbor and hate your enemy.' But I say to you, Love your enemies and pray for those who persecute you, so that you may be sons of your Father who is in heaven; for he makes his sun rise on the evil and on the good, and sends rain on the just and on the unjust" (Mt 5:43–45). We are to love all men and women, but not the world in so far as it opposes God. "Do not love the world or the things in the world. If any one loves the world, love for the Father is not in him" (1 Jn 2:15). Moreover, we should not forget that the world also opposes God in the measure that it disregards him: "The hand of our God is for good upon all that seek him, and the power of his wrath is against all

---

[1] John XXII, Papal Bull *In agro dominico* (March 27, 1329) condemning this proposition of Eckhart: DS 975.

that forsake him" (Ezr 8:22). Thus, we can understand Jesus' words: "He who is not with me is against me, and he who does not gather with me scatters" (Lk 11:23).

Love for the world

The world, indeed, is good, the fruit of the love of God, creator of all things. We read in Genesis: "And God saw everything he had made, and behold, it was very good" (Gn 1:31). "We must love the world and work and all human realities. For the world is good. Adam's sin destroyed the divine balance of creation; but God the Father sent his only Son to re establish peace, so that we, his children by adoption, might free creation from disorder and reconcile all things to God."[2]

But on contemplating the world and mankind, we should not lose sight of sin. We need only consider any epoch in history: Along with many positive aspects, we also find in men's heart and in their accomplishments an abundance of evil.

It is not true that everyone today—in general—is closed or indifferent to what our Christian faith teaches about man's being and destiny. It is not true that men in our time are turned only toward the things of this earth and have forgotten to look up to

---

[2] St. Josemaría, *Christ Is Passing By*, no. 112.

heaven. There is no lack of narrow ideologies, it is true, or of persons who maintain them. But in our time we find both great desires and base attitudes, heroism and cowardice, zeal and disenchantment: men who dream of a new world, more just and more human, and others who, discouraged perhaps by the failure of their youthful idealism, hide themselves in the selfishness of seeking only their own security or remaining immersed in their errors.[3]

Natural disasters, diseases, etc., which so often lead to human suffering, are also deeply rooted in the disorder the first sin introduced in the world. A love for what is disordered in man and in the world is an evil love, a false love.

Unity between love for God and love for neighbor

We have come to believe in God's love: in these words the Christian can express the fundamental decision in his or her life. Being Christian is not the result of an ethical choice or a lofty idea, but the encounter with an event, a person, which gives life a new horizon and a decisive direction. St. John's Gospel describes that event in these words: "God so loved the world that he gave his only Son, that whoever be-

[3] St. Josemaría, *Christ Is Passing By*, no. 132.

lieves in him should . . . have eternal life" (3:16). In acknowledging the centrality of love, Christian faith has retained the core of Israel's faith, while at the same time giving it new depth and breadth. The pious Jew prayed daily the words of the Book of Deuteronomy which expressed the heart of his existence: "Hear, O Israel: the Lord our God is one Lord, and you shall love the Lord your God with all your heart, and with all your soul and with all your might" (6:4–5). Jesus united into a single precept this commandment of love for God and the commandment of love for neighbor found in the Book of Leviticus: "You shall love your neighbor as yourself" (19:18; see Mk 12:29–31). Since God has first loved us (see 1 Jn 4:10), love is now no longer a mere "command"; it is the response to the gift of love with which God draws near to us.[4]

If the second commandment (loving our neighbor as ourselves) is taken as the only meaning of the first (loving God above all things); if love for God *were* love for neighbor, while setting aside God for all intents and purposes, then what would our love for ourselves be like? It would be not only a total love, but an absolute love, since we would make ourselves the absolute. But the one who loves himself with absolute love, would not

---

[4] Benedict XVI, *Deus caritas est*, no. 1.

be able to love his neighbor as himself, since the absolute is necessarily only one and excludes any other. In this contradiction, the marvelous harmony of authentic charity is broken. For charity enables us to love our neighbor with a total love (*to the end*), when we love God with an absolute love. Therefore, the denial of God, whether theoretical or practical, never results in a greater love for our neighbor, but rather in loving that person in the measure that he or she coincides with our self-love or proves useful in some manner. In the end, with God out of the picture, this frequently turns into hatred for everyone by everyone, the atmosphere suited to hell: There one finds the man who possesses himself, who loves what is exclusively his own and in some way infinite—the nothingness from which he comes.

It is possible to love other people uprightly, without explicitly loving God, since these persons are neither God nor part of God. But this love, in the end, is defined and limited by self-love: insofar as others are in a certain way part of oneself (by ties of blood, friendship, common interests, etc.). Although such love is positive, it nevertheless is imperfect; and above all, it cannot be offered unconditionally—or better, totally—to everyone. For as St. Augustine said so well: "Two cities have been formed by two loves: the earthly, by the love of self even to the contempt of God, and the heavenly, by the love of God even to the contempt of self. The former glories in itself, the latter, in God."[5]

Without explicitly rejecting God, some people seem to think that, in bygone ages and cultures, the Church's life consisted above all in making manifest God's glory and power and dominion over the world. Today, however, the new circumstances of a secularized world require emphasizing a hope in mankind's future, and therefore the universal fraternity of all human beings becomes the underlying premise required for God to be preached. This conscious, or unconscious, substitution of God by humanity is manifested in many different ways, with more or less explicit statements of secularization, and even leads to various forms of modern idolatry.

The complaint of the prophet Jeremiah is as relevant today as ever: "Be appalled, O heavens, at this, be shocked, be utterly desolate, says the Lord, for my people have committed two evils: they have forsaken me, the fountain of waters, and hewed out cisterns for themselves, broken cisterns, that can hold no water" (Jer 2:12:13).

We Christians cannot become prophets of doom, overlooking or failing to appreciate the good that, by God's mercy, is clearly seen in the world. Nor can we give in to despair, for our hope is not based on our own

[5] St. Augustine, *De civitate Dei*, bk. 14, c. 28: PL 41, 436. As of February 017, available at http://www.ccel.org/ccel/schaff/npnf102.iv.XIV.28.html.

strength or virtue, but on Christ Jesus, who assured us: "I am with you always, to the close of the age" (Mt 28:20); and on his promise that, in the face of difficulties that the Church would meet in the course of history, "the gates of hell shall not prevail against it" (Mt 16:19).

It is helpful to often consider carefully the supreme commandment of love for God, and the inseparable one of love for others.

> Love of God and love of neighbor are thus inseparable, they form a single commandment. But both live from the love of God who has loved us first. No longer is it a question, then, of a "commandment" imposed from without and calling for the impossible, but rather of a freely-bestowed experience of love from within, a love which by its very nature must then be shared with others. Love grows through love. Love is "divine" because it comes from God and unites us to God; through this unifying process it makes us a "we" which transcends our divisions and makes us one, until in the end God is "all in all" (1 Cor 15:28).[6]

Guided by the Word of God, we need to go deeper into the content and demands of the charity St. Paul describes in his letter to the Corinthians: "Love is patient and kind; love is not jealous or boastful; it is not arro-

---

[6] Benedict XVI, *Deus caritas est*, no. 18.

gant or rude. Love does not insist on its own way; it is not irritable or resentful; it does not rejoice at wrong, but rejoices in the right. Love bears all things, believes all things, hopes all things, endures all things" (1 Cor 13:4–7).

Part II

Loving God

Chapter 1

The Theological Virtues
and Christian Life

Let us once again listen to Jesus' reply to the question about the first and greatest commandment: "You shall love the Lord your God with all your heart, and with all your soul, and with all your mind. This is the great and first commandment" (Mt 22:37–38). Our Lord reaffirms here a natural obligation for all men and women and a divinely revealed precept from the Old Testament. Human nature itself requires this love as its proper and ultimate end, and living without it results in complete human frustration. For as St. Thomas says, all creatures have a natural inclination to love God more than themselves,[1] even though this can easily be lost sight of, and even stifled, owing to personal freedom.

Original sin, by introducing disorder and imbalance in human nature, weakened our natural inclination towards the supreme Good, divine Goodness. Thus, there appeared in the depths of the human heart a principle

[1] See St. Thomas, *Summa Theologiae*, I, q. 60, a. 5.

of opposition and resistance: "another law," which led St. Paul to exclaim, "I see in my members another law at war with the law of my mind and making me captive to the law of sin which dwells in my members" (Rom 7:23).

Therefore, it was fitting that God himself should reveal in a supernatural way, by his own word, not only the mysteries that are strictly supernatural, completely surpassing human understanding, but also the principal religious truths of the natural order, so that these could be easily known by all, with firm certainty and without admixture of error.[2] The commandment to love God, like all the other commandments making explicit and applying this first one, is before all else part of revelation: It is the word of God guiding our human path in life, and a sign of his love that wants all men and women to come to know and love him, and by loving him, to attain their complete and eternal happiness.

But God, in his infinite goodness and mercy, has willed that the natural love we owe him as creatures should be transformed into supernatural charity—into love for God the Father, proper to God the Son and to those who have been raised up to participate in his supernatural filiation. This is the love the Holy Spirit infuses in our hearts (see Rom 5:5), so that we, by being

---

[2] See Vatican Council I, Dogmatic Constitution on the Catholic Faith *Dei Filius* (April 24, 1870), chap. 2. As of February 2017, available at https://www.ewtn.com/library/COUNCILS/V1.htm .

united to the Only Begotten Son, to Christ, may be transformed from servants into sons and daughters, from strangers into members of God's household (see Eph 2:19). "In Christ, taught by him, we dare to call God our Father—he is the Almighty who created heaven and earth, and he is a loving Father who waits for us to come back to him again and again, as the story of the prodigal son repeats itself in our lives."[3]

Life of faith

Love for God presupposes faith, just as the will, analogously, presupposes knowledge. Faith, St. Paul teaches the Galatians, works through love (see Gal 5:6), and without faith we would not be able to please God (see Heb 11:6). This faith refers directly to God: It is a *theological* virtue that leads us to *believe in God* and to *believe God*. The act of faith, although a form of knowledge and formally rooted in the intellect, also involves the entire person. Latin terminology adequately expresses three aspects of the act of faith that are closely intertwined: *credere Deum*, insofar as God himself is the *object* that is principally believed; *credere Deo*, since the motive for believing is God himself: We believe all that God tells us. These two aspects, clearly intellectual in nature, are united to a third aspect, *credere in Deum*, which expresses

---

[3] St. Josemaría, *Christ Is Passing By*, no. 91.

the function of the will moving the intellect to assent to the revealed truth, insofar as this truth, God himself, has for the will the aspect of an end. Faith, therefore, means to *believe in God*, to *believe God* and to *believe unto God*.[4] Supernatural faith involves not only knowledge but also each person's self-giving to God, who gives himself to us in his Revelation.

> Faith is born of an encounter with the living God who calls us and reveals his love, a love which precedes us and upon which we can lean for security and for building our lives. Transformed by this love, we gain fresh vision, new eyes to see; we realize that it contains a great promise of fulfillment, and that a vision of the future opens up before us. Faith, received from God as a supernatural gift, becomes a light for our way, guiding our journey through time.[5]

We can and should believe also other revealed truths that do not seem at first sight to refer directly to God (for example, the immortality of the human soul), even though our natural reason can arrive at this truth by its

[4] See St. Thomas, *Summa Theologiae*, II-II, q. 2, a. 2.
[5] Pope Francis, Encyclical Letter on Faith *Lumen fidei* (June 29, 2013), no. 4. As of February 2017, available at http://w2.vatican.va/content/francesco/en/encyclicals/documents/papa-francesco_20130629_enciclica-lumen-fidei.html.

own power. But even then, it is a question of believing with *theological* faith, which necessarily refers to God. As St. Thomas explains:

> Although there are many articles of faith, some of which refer to the divinity, others to the humanity the Son of God assumed in the unity of Person, and still others to the effects of the divine nature; nevertheless, the foundation of all faith is the first truth itself of the divinity, since all the other truths are contained under faith insofar as they are, in some way, reducible to God. Thus the Lord says to his disciples: "*Creditis in Deum, et in me credite*—You believe in God, believe also in me" (Jn 14:1), thereby indicating that we believe in Christ insofar as he is God, as faith principally about God.[6]

Faith, the necessary requirement for supernatural charity, is also a gift from God: "For by grace you have been saved through faith; and this is not your own doing, it is the gift of God" (Eph 2:4). It is an unmerited grace, a supernatural virtue, which we need to guard like a treasure. When our faith falters, from the depths of our soul should come, before all else, that humble petition the Apostles addressed to Jesus: "*Adauge nobis fidem!*—increase our faith!" (Lk 17:5).

---

[6] St. Thomas Aquinas, *Expositio primae decretalis*, 1.

Christian hope

Faith and charity bring with them hope, also a theological virtue since its object is God himself. Christian hope is grounded not on our own strength but on God's power and faithfulness to his promises. And like faith and charity, hope is a supernatural virtue God infuses with his grace.[7] It is a hope not for something fleeting or perishable, but the joyous hope for full and definitive happiness in heaven, where "death shall be no more, neither shall there be mourning, nor crying nor pain any more, for the former things have passed away" (Rv 21:4).

"If God is for us, who is against us?" (Rom 8:31). This firm assurance is based on the Christian hope of definitively sharing in God's glory; Thus, it can provide us with a deeply serene and joyful vision of our life and of human history, despite our own frailty and the spectacle of human weaknesses. It is the only and true reason for our assurance, even amid the most adverse circumstances, that "in everything God works for good with those who love him" (Rom 8:28).

Our hope in the hereafter does not lead a Christian to be unconcerned about the here and now. On the con-

---

[7] On charity's relationship with faith and hope, see Paul O'Callaghan, *Children of God in the World: An Introduction to Theological Anthropology* (Washington D.C.: The Catholic University of America Press, 2016), pp. 417–419.

trary, it enables and spurs us to appreciate and love all human realities, and to recognize their true meaning. "Authentic Christianity, which professes the resurrection of all flesh, has always quite logically opposed 'disincarnation,' without fear of being judged materialistic. We can, therefore, rightfully speak of a 'Christian materialism,' which is boldly opposed to that materialism which is blind to the spirit."[8]

[8] St. Josemaría Escrivá, *Conversations with St. Josemaría Escrivá* (New York: Scepter Publishers, 2003), no. 115.

Chapter 2

Consequences of the Secularization of Christianity

The secularization of charity that, in theory or practice, reduces love for God to love for neighbor, brings with it the secularization of faith. For what would faith mean in the life of a person who, in one way or another, completely replaces God with an anthropocentric world view?

Nevertheless, not a few people have come to consider faith as merely a commitment to human progress, in the social, economic, political, or educational spheres. Then evangelizing action, the effort to stir up people's faith, is inevitably reduced to human aspirations and problems. Such faith would only be meaningful as a *factor of change* for a more just and human society. And the doctrinal content of faith would become the object of continual revision and critical reflection according to the signs of the times. This concept of the faith is not far from the Lutheran one, since what God is *in himself* would be of little importance: the only really important thing would be what, in any given historical epoch, he means *for us*. Thus, the word of God is set aside, his revelation is rejected, his image fades, and man is left alone with himself.

Blessed Paul VI wrote that "there are in fact profound links"[1] between evangelization and human advancement, since we need to consider the human person in the unity of all the dimensions that grace raises up to the supernatural plane. At the same time, this Pontiff also reminded us:

> The Church links human liberation and salvation in Jesus Christ, but she never identifies them, because she knows through revelation, historical experience and the reflection of faith that not every notion of liberation is necessarily consistent and compatible with an evangelical vision of man, of things and of events; she knows too that in order that God's kingdom should come it is not enough to establish liberation and to create well-being and development.[2]

Faith and being faithful

The Second Vatican Council reminded us that "the Christian economy, therefore, since it is the new and

---

[1] Bl. Paul VI, Apostolic Exhortation on Evangelization in the Modern World *Evangelii nuntiandi* (December 8, 1975), no. 31. As of February 2017, available at http://w2.vatican.va/content/paul-vi/en/apost_exhortations/documents/hf_p-vi_exh_19751208_evangelii-nuntiandi.html.

[2] Paul VI, *Evangelii nuntiandi*, no. 35.

definitive covenant, will never pass away; and no new public revelation is to be expected before the glorious manifestation of our Lord, Jesus Christ."[3] So being faithful is one of the fundamental Christian attitudes: being faithful to what has been received (see 1 Tm 6:20), to what is not ours but God's, and to what God has entrusted to all men and women of all times. Thus, faith is totally different from any merely human knowledge. Although the faith we profess no longer allows for anything new in its content, nevertheless, due to our temporal existence, it does allow over time for a homogenous development and an ever-deeper grasp and understanding of its content. And therefore, as long as fidelity to the immutable content of revealed truth is preserved (which is fidelity to God), it is licit, and sometimes necessary, to adapt this content to the language of the people to whom the announcement of the faith is addressed, today and now.

Although this effort isn't easy, it shouldn't be neglected. Nor should we forget that the tie between language and the signified reality is considerably closer than might at first seem to be the case. It is not surprising, then, that the precise concepts and formulas used to

[3] Vatican Council II, Dogmatic Constitution on Divine Revelation *Dei Verbum* (November 18, 1965), no. 4. As of February 2017, available at http://www.vatican.va/archive/hist_councils/ii_vatican_council/documents/vat-ii_const_19651118_dei-verbum_en.html.

express the truths of faith have been taken up by the Magisterium of the Church, and that, as Pius XII taught, "it is wrong to depart from them."[4]

The existence of immutable truths is, of itself, evident. Unless one views man, the fluctuating human consciousness, as the foundation and measure of the reality of things, one needs to acknowledge that things are as they are and that something is true insofar as it is. Hence, where there is no change in being, there is no change in its truth. And thus "the object of faith cannot change over time, while the evolution of all human science unfolds in mankind's history."[5]

Fidelity to the faith is fidelity, loyalty, to God. We do not believe something because it is old or new, but because it has been taught to us by God, who also enables us to accept it. Our faith, as St. Thomas says, is not an "opinion strengthened by reasons;"[6] it always requires a humble submission and obedience to God's majesty: "the obedience of faith" (Rom 1:5). In contrast, if faith is understood to refer essentially and primarily to man and this world, it would not be faith at all, but just one

---

[4] Pius XII, Encyclical Letter concerning Some False Opinions Which Threaten to Undermine the Foundations of Catholic Doctrine *Humani generis* (August 12, 1950), no. 16. As of February 2017, available at http://w2.vatican.va/content/pius-xii/en/encyclicals/documents/hf_p-xii_enc_12081950_humani-generis.html.

[5] Paul VI, *Allocution*, September 7, 1966.

[6] St. Thomas Aquinas, *In Sententia*, Prologue, q. 1, a. 3, qla. 3. 3, sol. 3.

more ideology, open to change because of its fleeting and ephemeral nature.

Christian truth is life and way

The Christian truth is not a simply a collection of abstract statements; it is not sufficient to *know* the truth—we need to live it. We only really know the truth when it becomes life in us. And this is the truth that makes us free: *veritas liberabit vos* (Jn 8:32). In coming to know it we come to love it, and in loving it we are freed from the slavery of sin. This truth is Christ himself: a Truth that is also the Way and the Life. "*Ego sum via, veritas et vita*—I am the way, the truth and the life" (Jn 14:6). As Thomas Aquinas said, "Just as a person who has a book containing all knowledge would seek only to learn what is in that book, so we too need only seek Christ."[7]

Faith is the foundation of hope (see Heb 11:1). Therefore the "secularization" of the faith also lowers Christian hope to the level of this world. Reduced to hope in a future world that is more human and just, the hope described by St. Paul can be overlooked: "What no eye has seen, nor ear heard, nor the heart of man conceived, what God has prepared for those who love him" (1 Cor 2:9).

---

[7] St. Thomas Aquinas, *In Epistula ad Colossenses*, c. 2, lec. 1.

This secularization of the faith has gone so far, for example, as to reinterpret Christ's Ascension. What this event actually meant for Jesus is viewed as unimportant. The important thing is to see his Ascension as a symbol and an invitation to us to "ascend," to rise up, to make progress, to rebel against oppression. But for such a mundane enterprise, there is really no need to have recourse to Christian motives. The next step, which unfortunately some have taken, is quite predictable: If God is exclusively a motive for desiring and seeking a more just and happy future in this world, then he would truly become superfluous. With our hope centered on a future incapable of satisfying the aspirations of the human spirit, and faced with unmistakable evidence of its utopian nature, mankind would end up enclosed in itself, in its own desolate indigence and hopelessness.

In the forgetfulness or even rejection of the ultimate goal of our hope, eternal life, we can also sometimes find the limitations our imagination faces in grasping the concept of eternity. As Benedict XVI said in one of his encyclicals:

"Eternal," in fact, suggests to us the idea of something interminable, and this frightens us; "life" makes us think of the life that we know and love and do not want to lose, even though very often it brings more toil than satisfaction, so that while on the one hand we desire it, on the other hand we do not want it. To imagine ourselves outside the temporality that imprisons us and in some way to sense that eternity is not an unending succession of days in the calendar, but something more like the supreme moment of satisfaction, in which totality embraces us and we embrace totality—this we can only attempt. It would be like plunging into the ocean of infinite love, a moment in which time—the before and after—no longer exists. We can only attempt to grasp the idea that such a moment is life in the full sense, a plunging ever anew into the vastness of being, in which we are simply overwhelmed with joy. This is how Jesus expresses it in St. John's Gospel: "I will see you again and your hearts will rejoice, and no one will take your joy from you" (16:22). We must think along these lines if we want to understand the object of Christian hope, to understand what it is that our faith, our being with Christ, leads us to expect."[8]

Moral life: love and freedom

Freedom is a natural gift, proper to a spiritual nature. But pure nature does not exist. After our first parents' fall, all men and women exist either in the state of supernatural grace or in the state of sin. Since Christ is the one who frees us from sin, "man cannot be fully under-

[8] Benedict XVI, *Spe salvi*, no. 12.

stood without Christ. Or rather, man is incapable of understanding himself fully without Christ. He cannot understand who he is, nor what his true dignity is, nor what his vocation is, nor what his final end is. He cannot understand any of this without Christ."[9]

Human freedom also needs to be redeemed: it not only needs to be healed in its natural dimension but also raised up to the supernatural order and turned into a new freedom.

> Where does our freedom come from? It comes from Christ our Lord. This is the freedom with which he has ransomed us (see Gal 4:31). That is why he teaches, "if the Son makes you free, you will be free indeed" (Jn 8:36). We Christians do not have to ask anyone to tell us the true meaning of this gift, because the only freedom that can save man is Christian freedom.[10]

Christ is the Way, the Truth and the Life (see Jn 14:16). The relationship between freedom, love, and truth acquires a new dimension beyond the natural dependence of the will on the intellect. "*Veritas liberabit vos*— the truth will make you free" (Jn 8:32).

[9] St. John Paul II, *Homily*, June 2, 1979. As of February 2017, available at http://w2.vatican.va/content/john-paul-ii/en/homilies/1979/documents/hf_jp-ii_hom_19790602_polonia-varsavia.html.

[10] St. Josemaría, *Friends of God*, no. 35.

How great a truth is this, which opens the way to freedom and gives it meaning throughout our lives. I will sum it up for you, with the joy and certainty which flow from knowing there is a close relationship between God and his creatures. It is the knowledge that we have come from the hands of God, that the Blessed Trinity looks upon us with predilection, that we are children of so wonderful a Father. I ask my Lord to help us decide to take this truth to heart, to dwell upon it day by day; only then will we be acting as free men. Do not forget: anyone who does not realize that he is a child of God is unaware of the deepest truth about himself. When he acts he lacks the dominion and selfmastery we find in those who love our Lord above all else.[11]

The knowledge of the truth that frees us is not merely intellectual. The truth of our divine filiation is essentially Christ himself (see Jn 14:6), for we are *sons in the Son.* And this liberating knowledge, which is faith, is expressed in love: the act proper to freedom. It is "faith working through love" (Gal 5:6).

Faith, hope, and love, by providing intrinsic meaning and direction, configure the Christian's moral life, which is centered and grounded on love for God and

---

[11] St. Josemaría, *Friends of God*, no. 26.

neighbor. It is the morality of God's children, not of slaves. The Christian vocation is a vocation to freedom: "*in libertatem vocati estis*—you were called to freedom" (Gal 5:13), St. Paul writes to the Galatians. And the freedom to which we are called is not just any sort of freedom, but the *freedom of God's children*: the freedom that comes from loving God. A person who loves God, in the measure that he or she truly does so, wants what God wants. And the moral law then is seen not as a coercion or an obstacle to our desires, but rather as a sure path towards Love, and therefore towards freedom and personal fulfilment.

On the relationship between love and freedom, perhaps the most concise and profound formula is that of St. Augustine: "*Dilige, et quod vis fac*—Love, and do what you will."[12] As the Bishop of Hippo also wrote, whoever does the good moved by charity is not subject to necessity, since "freedom belongs to charity—*quia libertas est caritatis.*"[13] Thomas Aquinas expressed the same truth in these words: "*Quanto aliquis plus habet de caritate, plus habet de libertate*—The more charity someone has, the freer he is."[14]

Freedom belongs to charity because freedom is the capacity to love what is good for its own sake, and also

[12] St. Augustine, *In Epistolam Ioannis ad parthos*, 7, 8: PL. 35, 2033.

[13] St. Augustine, *De natura et gratia*, 65, 78: PL 44, 286.

[14] St. Thomas Aquinas, *In III Sent.*, d. 29, q. 1, a. 8, qla. 3.

because the basis for the possibility of choosing between different goods is the will's constitutive orientation toward the good, and this orientation finds its full realization only in one's love for God. Besides, charity should imbue every corner of the life of Christ's disciples, so that everything is done for love. And it is impossible to love unless one loves freely, since love is the act proper to freedom. Although the Gospel is a law, the New Law, it is easy to understand why St. James in his epistle calls it "the perfect law, the law of liberty" (Jas 1:25). Everything is summed up in the law of love, not only as an external norm commanding us to love, but also as an interior grace giving us the strength to love. As St. Thomas said: "The New Law is chiefly the grace itself of the Holy Spirit, which is given to those who believe."[15]

> Love of God marks out the path of truth, justice and goodness. When we make up our minds to tell our Lord, "I put my freedom in your hands," we find ourselves loosed from the many chains that were binding us to insignificant things, ridiculous cares or petty ambitions. Then our freedom, which is a treasure beyond price, a wonderful pearl that it would be a tragedy to cast before swine (see Mt 7:6), will be used by us entirely to learn how to do good

---

[15] St. Thomas, *Summa Theologiae*, I-II, q. 106, a. 1 c.

(see Is 1:17). This is the glorious freedom of the children of God.[16]

However, "as long as we are on this earth, we will never achieve complete freedom."[17] In eternal life, in glory, where we will no longer have the possibility of choosing between good and evil, not only will we continue to be free, but our freedom will be the fullest possible. "Only when we love do we attain the fullest freedom: the freedom of not wanting ever to abandon, for all eternity, the object of our love."[18]

Secularization of moral life

The secularization of faith, hope, and love for God necessarily leads to a secularization of moral life: judging human behavior with merely earthly criteria, while rejecting the horizon of faith. Having strayed from the only right path, the end result can only be to fall into subjectivism: trying to understand mankind and the world but setting aside any firm metaphysical and anthropological principles. The categories of human history are appealed to, but in an uncritical way; it is a history that looks not to the past or present, but only to the future. "When the culture itself is corrupt and objective

[16] St. Josemaría, *Friends of God*, no. 38.
[17] St. Josemaría, *Friends of God*, no. 36.
[18] St. Josemaría, *Friends of God*, no. 38.

truth and universally valid principles are no longer up-
held, then laws can only be seen as arbitrary impositions
or obstacles to be avoided."[19]

The positing of man as the ultimate standard for judging good and evil cannot but recall the diabolical temptation addressed to our first parents: "Your will be like
God, knowing good and evil" (Gn 3:5). But the Holy
Spirit, in the powerful words of St. Paul, warns us what
man achieves when he doesn't want to acknowledge
God:

> For although they knew God they did not honor
> him as God or give thanks to him, but they became
> futile in their thinking and their senseless minds
> were darkened. Claiming to be wise, they became
> fools. . . . Therefore God gave them up in the lusts
> of their hearts to impurity, to the dishonoring to
> their bodies among themselves, because they ex-
> changed the truth about God for a lie and wor-
> shipped and served the creature rather than the
> Creator, who is blessed forever! Amen. For this rea-
> son God gave them up to dishonorable passions . . .
> to a base mind and to improper conduct. They were
> filled with all manner of wickedness, evil, covetous-
> ness, malice. Full of envy, murder, strife, deceit, ma-
> lignity, they are gossips, slanderers, haters of God,

[19] Francis, *Laudato si*, no. 123.

insolent, haughty, boastful, inventors of evil, disobe-
dient to parents, foolish, faithless, heartless, ruth-
less. (Rom 1:21–31)

The rejection of God turns wisdom into foolishness; injustice proliferates and human beings profane their
own body through impurity. Not believing in God, certainly, does not always lead to a life like the one St. Paul
describes. Nevertheless, without a transcendent foundation, without God, it becomes impossible to defend co-
herently the existence of objective and immutable moral norms, and moral subjectivism or relativism rears its
head.

Chapter 3

What Loving God Requires

The love God asks of us is a total, absolute love: *ex tota virtute, ex tota mente.* The absolute character of this love is not hard to grasp: It must be unconditional, not admitting anything foreign to God. A love for God without any conditions implies, for example, that we should love him in any and every circumstance: in prosperity and adversity; in health and sickness; in peace and war; in joy and sorrow; when external expressions of this love are popular, and when they lead to persecution and even death; and even when loving God provokes painful splits in family relationships, between friends, etc.

St. Augustine, pointing to the total love we owe God, told his preaching audience: "What is left of your heart for loving yourself? What is left of your soul, and of your mind? He says 'the whole.' He who made you requires you to give yourself completely."[1] We should love God *totally*, not partially—not as one among other objects of

[1] St. Augustine, *Sermon* 34, 4, 7: PL 38, 212.

our love, nor even as the most important one. Love for God should encompass and embrace, and also ground, all our other loves: our love for ourselves and for others. "Jesus is never satisfied 'sharing.' He wants all."[2]

This supernatural love is totally opposed to a disincarnate, cold, and inhuman spiritualism. "You are afraid of becoming distant and cold with everyone. You want so much to be detached! Get rid of that fear. If you belong to Christ—completely to Christ—he will give you fire, light and warmth for everyone."[3]

This total love for God has some particular characteristics. Loving God totally—Father, Son, and Holy Spirit—means first of all also loving everything that refers to God: the Most Holy Humanity of Christ, especially; and then our Lady, God's Mother; and also the Church. St. Cyprian wrote in the year 251: "He cannot have God for his Father who does not have the Church for his Mother."[4] A person does not truly love God who does not love the Church. And likewise, a person does not totally love God who does not love all that God loves: every created being.

In second place, we can and should love God totally insofar as this love, as was said above, embraces and grounds all our other loves. In third place, loving God

---

[2] St. Josemaría, *The Way*, no. 155.

[3] St. Josemaría, *The Way*, no. 154.

[4] St. Cyprian, *De Catholicae Ecclesiae unitate*, 6: PL 4, 502.

totally should mean loving him as much as he can be loved. But this exceeds our possibilities, since God is infinite and cannot be fathomed by any creature.

We can't love God too much

To "miss the mark," to sin by having too much charity, or too much faith and hope, is strictly speaking impossible:

> The measure and the rule for theological virtue is God himself; his truth for our faith, his goodness for our charity, his sheer omnipotence and loving-kindness for our hope. This measure surpasses all human power, so that we can never love God as much as he ought to be loved, nor believe and hope in him as much as we should. Much less, therefore, can there be excess here.[5]

But we should never stop striving to grow in our love, which is always possible and necessary. Although we can never love him as much as he can and should be loved, this shouldn't stop us from trying: "Lord, may I have weight and measure in everything . . . except in Love."[6]

Perhaps we might at times think it is hard to love God, if love is viewed as a heartfelt sentiment, as a feeling of affection. And this might lead us to conclude that love

[5] St. Thomas, *Summa Theologiae*, I-II, q. 64, a. 4.
[6] St. Josemaria, *The Way*, no. 427.

for God is a matter of the will alone, not of feelings. Nevertheless, loving God totally entails loving him with all our capacity to love: with our feelings too.

> The principle of love is two-fold, for a man can love both by sentiment and by a dictate of reason: by sentiment, when he does not know how to live without the beloved; and by dictate of reason, when he loves what his understanding tells him. We should love God in both ways, also with our feeling, so that our heart of flesh feels moved by God, in accord with what is said in the Psalm (83:3): "my heart and my flesh rejoice in the living God."[7]

We have to love God with our will and our feelings. Charity is not a cold, dry affair. God asks for our whole heart, with all its possibilities of loving: with a firm will that follows the dictate of reason, and with our affections:

> Note that God does not say: "In exchange for our own heart, I will give you a will of pure spirit." No, he gives us a heart, a human heart, like Christ's. I don't have one heart for loving God and another for loving people. I love Christ and the Father and the Holy Spirit and our Lady with the same heart with which I love my parents and my friends. I shall

---

[7] St. Thomas Aquinas, *Super Evangelium S. Matthaei Lectura*, 22, 4.

never tire of repeating that. We must be very human, for otherwise we cannot be divine.[8]

We might think it impossible to love God like this, seeing him apparently so distant, so far removed from us. But God himself has completely overcome this difficulty. He has become man in Jesus Christ, so that through him, with him and in him we can also love the Father and the Holy Spirit. "He who has seen me has seen the Father" (Jn 14:9). By contemplating God in Christ, who loves us with a human heart, we learn how to love—also with our feelings—the Blessed Trinity.

Love for God: worship and prayer

Love for God, like all true love, is not only a sentiment. It is far removed from empty sentimentality, for it has to spur us to undertake many specific deeds. It is a love that should encompass and guide every corner of our life. In first place, it requires of us *worship, adoration, giving glory to God*, not because God "needs" the glory we render him, but because we owe it to him. Since we are creatures, it couldn't be otherwise. To the extent that we lovingly adore and glorify God, we attain our ultimate end of complete happiness. In divine worship, "the glory is for God and the benefit for us men."[9] This

[8] St. Josemaría, *Christ Is Passing By*, no. 166.
[9] St. Thomas, *Summa Theologiae*, II-II, q. 81, a. 6 ad 2.

harmony and inseparability between God's glory and the good of mankind was announced by the angels at the birth of the Man-God: "*Gloria in altissimis Deo, et in terra pax hominibus bonae voluntatis*—Glory to God in the highest; and on earth peace to men of good will" (Lk 2:14). The inspired word of Sirach exhorts us: "When you praise the Lord, exalt him as much as you can: for he will surpass even that" (43:30).

Although we need to dedicate specific moments of our life exclusively to giving glory to God, we shouldn't view this as just another activity among others, for the ultimate aim of all our actions should be to give God glory: "So, whether you eat or drink, or whatever you do, do all to the glory of God" (1 Cor 10:31).

Present in our worship of God, also when carried out externally in the liturgy, is the internal reality of our personal prayer. Prayer is one of the main expressions of our religious makeup, rooted in human nature itself. But this natural reality is elevated to the supernatural order in Christian prayer, which gives expression to the reality of our divine filiation.[10] Divine filiation marks every aspect of a Christian's life and actions. Christian prayer is characterized not only by its filial nature— approaching God with the trust and affection of children. It gives expression to the existential reality that we

[10] On specifically Christian prayer, see, for example, Fernando Ocariz, *Naturaleza, gracia y gloria* (Pamplona: Eunsa, 2nd ed. 2002), pp. 273–281.

are God's children, sharers in the sonship of Christ, the eternal Word. Being children of God means to share in the same unique relationship that Christ enjoys with God the Father, which makes it possible for us to address God the Father as *Abba!* As St. Paul says: "you have received the Spirit of sonship, [whereby] we cry: 'Abba! Father!'" (Rom 8:15).

Prayer is meant to be a permanent reality in our life, just as our participation in the filiation of the eternal Word, of Christ, is permanent in our soul in grace. Hence the need "always to pray" (Lk 18:1), to "be constant in prayer" (Rom 12:12). With God's grace and charity, this is possible to attain, because our deeds can also become prayer,[11] through a permanent orientation of our freedom, of our love, towards God.

Thus, Christian life, based on the theological virtues and therefore centered on God, is not meant to be something part-time, lived only when at church, at the margin of our ordinary life in the world. St. Josemaría insisted on this truth with special clarity and forcefulness:

> Your daily encounter with Christ takes place where your fellow men, your yearnings, your work, and your affections are. It is in the midst of the most material things of the earth that we must sanctify ourselves, serving God and all mankind. . . . Don't

[11] See St. Josemaría, *Friends of God*, no. 67.

doubt it, my children: any attempt to escape from the honest realities of daily life is, for you men and women of the world, something opposed to the will of God.

On the contrary, you must realize now, more clearly than ever, that God is calling you to serve him *in and from* the ordinary, secular and civil activities of human life. He waits for us every day, in the laboratory, in the operating theater, in the army barracks, in the university chair, in the factory, in the workshop, in the fields, in the home, and in all the immense panorama of work. Understand this well: there is something holy, something divine hidden in the most ordinary situations, and it is up to each one of you to discover it.[12]

Adoration of God, acknowledgement of his grandeur and of our own indigence, with heartfelt acts of thanksgiving because we have received everything from him—it is thus that we echo David's prayer: "all things come from you, and of your own have we given you" (1 Chr 29:14).

Love for God and obedience to his commandments

Another inseparable aspect of love for God is the observance of his commandments: "For this is the love of God, that we keep his commandments" (1 Jn 5:3).

[12] St. Josemaría, *Conversations with St. Josemaría Escrivá*, nos. 113–114.

Christ himself taught us this truth in very expressive terms: "Whoever does the will of God is my brother, and sister, and mother" (Mk 3:35); and also: "If a man loves me, he will keep my word" (Jn 14:23). The commandments of God's law, his will for us, are an expression of his love that guides us along our path in life; therefore, to keep them is to accept his love. "True liberation consists in opening oneself to the love of Christ. In him, and only in him, are we set free from all alienation and doubt, from slavery to the power of sin and death. Christ is truly 'our peace' (Eph 2:14); 'the love of Christ impels us' (2 Cor 5:14), giving meaning and joy to our life."[13]

Charity is a love with deeds, and these deeds are primarily the faithful fulfillment of all that God has commanded: "Not every one who says to me, 'Lord, Lord,' shall enter the kingdom of heaven, but he who does the will of my Father who is in heaven" (Mt 7:21). It is by spending our life loving God that we "will receive the crown of life which God has promised to those who love him" (Jas 1:12).

Love for God necessarily entails love for other people, since the totality of the love we owe God requires that we love everything he loves. Therefore, we ought to try to make life pleasant for others, but without forgetting that we ought first to please God. Hence the fundamen-

[13] St. John Paul II, *Redemptoris missio*, no. 11.

tal attitude of adoration and loving submission to God should give rise, first of all, to the real and sincere intention, shown in our deeds, of pleasing God, not men: "Am I now seeking the favor of men, or of God? Or am I trying to please men? If I were still pleasing men, I should not be a servant of Christ" (Gal 1:10).

Not seeking men's approval but God's. How different this attitude is from that which, as the main condition for preaching the Gospel, stresses the need to make it acceptable to modern man! The right approach is just the opposite: trying to convince modern man to accept what God approves, without being surprised that this is often hard to achieve. No one has ever announced the Gospel with greater force, clarity, and fervor than Christ did, and yet only a small number of people accepted and followed it. This was the case, for example, in Capernaum, when many of Jesus' followers left him after the discourse on the bread of life (see Jn 6:66). It would be misguided to think that the future of Christianity depends on successfully adapting the Christian message to the modern world. Rather it depends, as far as our own efforts are concerned, on each and every Christian striving for personal holiness, for identification with Christ. Ever timely are these words pointing to the right solution: "these world crises are crises of saints."[14]

[14] St. Josemaría, *The Way*, no. 301.

Love for God and personal conversion

Even when healed and raised up by grace, our human weakness is all too obvious, as our own and others' experience attests to. Therefore, sincere love for God includes the effective desire for conversion. This conversion is not only a matter of going from unbelief to faith, from sin to grace, from evil to good, but of making progress in leading a virtuous life. The goal of conversion is full identification with Christ, becoming ipse Christus. And hence conversion has to be a permanent attitude in our life, since we will always have the need to grow in this identification.

Moreover, "if we say we have no sin, we deceive ourselves, and the truth is not in us" (1 Jn 1:8). Therefore, spiritual progress towards identification with Christ, towards holiness, always includes a true conversion: asking God to forgive our sins and making the sincere effort to amend our ways, as Jesus himself taught us in the Our Father.

The experience of our weakness and sin, and the resulting need for conversion, should not give a sad or disillusioned tone to our spiritual life. For over and above our weakness is the merciful strength of God's love for us, marvelously presented by Jesus in the Parable of the Prodigal Son (see Lk 15:11–32). The "awareness that God is our Father brings joy to our conversion."[15]

---

[15] St. Josemaría, *Christ Is Passing By*, no. 64. See Javier Echevarría, *Paths of Interior Life* (New York: Scepter Publishers, 2010), p 127.

Idolatry

The first and greatest of the commandments is broken to the extent someone has an absolute and total love for himself, for mankind, or for any creature. In its many different forms and degrees, this is the sin of idolatry, which rejects the first precept of the Decalogue:

> You shall have no other gods before me. You shall not make for yourself a graven image, or any likeness of anything that is in heaven above, or that is in the earth beneath, or that is in the water under the earth; you shall not bow down to them or serve them; for I the Lord your God am a jealous God, visiting the iniquity of the fathers upon the children to the third and the fourth generation of those who hate me, but showing steadfast love to thousands of those who love me and keep my commandments. (Ex 20:3–6)

Sacred Scripture presents God's punishment of idolatry in powerful terms: "Whoever sacrifices to any god, save to the Lord only, shall be utterly destroyed" (Ex 22:20). Particularly harsh is the reprimand against the idolatry of whoever would try to use the word of God to justify their transgression. This is not the idolatry that fabricates idols of gold or silver, but the interior idolatry of those who have erected idols in their heart. Ezekiel's prophetic words show us God's reprimand against such idolaters:

> For any one of the house of Israel or of the strangers that sojourn in Israel, who separates himself from me, taking his idols into his heart and putting the stumbling block of his iniquity before his face, and yet comes to a prophet to inquire for himself of me, I the Lord will answer him myself: and I will set my face against that man, I will make him a sign and a byword and cut him off from the midst of my people; and you shall know that I am the Lord. (Ez 14:7–8)

These words, certainly harsh, are not without relevance for our own day and age. They can well be applied to those who, in every epoch, have sought support in the Gospel (or in the "prophet" who teaches it) for an interior idolatry they are not prepared to renounce. Ezekiel's words are also a strong warning against the ever-present temptation of "making easy," compatible with idols, the great demands of love for God—a love that should be "as strong as death" (Song 8:6).

To take God's place, man can find many "idols." But in the end they always turn out to be man himself. Since the main object of our love is also the main object of our hope, the prophet Jeremiah writes forcefully about those who place their hope not in God but in man: "Thus says the Lord: 'Cursed is the man who trusts in man and makes flesh his arm, whose heart turns away from the Lord'" (Jer 17:5). Obviously, God doesn't require that we distrust others, or that we see ourselves as self-sufficient, needing no help from our fellow men. On the contrary, the theological virtue of hope also refers to creatures; but only as the secondary object, not the principal one.

Worship of God and human fraternity

The precept of love is also broken when we fail to render God the worship he is due; and therefore, when we find the goal, center, or principal object of liturgical ceremonies in human realities (the community, for example). Fraternity among men is truly Christian, not when it is limited to the "horizontal plane," but when it stems primarily from the personal union of each of us with Christ Jesus. The sacrament of the Church's unity is the Holy Eucharist. By participating in the Sacrifice of Christ and growing in union with him, each Christian is identified more closely with and becomes more fully a member of the same Body, the Church, through an ever-closer union with its Head: Christ Jesus. For "the Church is the People of God, who live from the Body of Christ and become the very Body of Christ in the celebration of the Eucharist."[16]

---

[16] Joseph Ratzinger, *Zeichen unter den Völkern, in Wahreit un Zeugnis*, ed. Michael Schmaus and Alfred Läpple (Desseldorf: Patmos, 1964), p. 459.

This external worship is obligatory not only for each person; it also "binds the whole community of human beings, grouped together by mutual social ties: mankind, too, depends on the sovereign authority of God."[17] Hence, in reference to public worship, the precept of love for God is broken when people lose sight of the divine, and service to our fellow men is seen as the primary and essential element of religion. When adoration and sacrifice (a total self-offering to God) are no longer viewed as essential to religion, both natural and supernatural, it is easy to forget that dedication to God involves not only the inner world, but also the riches of the material world. The claim can even be made that dedicating places and objects exclusively to God is unchristian (the richness of churches would become an "anti-sign" of evangelical poverty). But as the Gospel recounts:

> That woman in the house of Simon the leper in Bethany, who anoints the Master's head with precious ointment, reminds us of our duty to be generous in the worship of God. All beauty, richness and majesty seem little to me. And against those who attack the richness of sacred vessels, of vestments and

[17] St. Pius XII, Encyclical on Communion with the Holy See *Mediator Dei* (November 20, 1947), no. 14. As of February 2017, available at http://w2.vatican.va/content/pius-xii/en/encyclicals/documents/hf_p-xii_enc_20111947_mediator-dei.html.

altars, stands the praise given by Jesus: "*opus enim bonum operata est in me*—she has acted well towards me."[18]

Let us not forget that Judas, referring to the poor, criticized that woman's gesture, while Christ in contrast praised her and made sure that her example would always be remembered (see Mt 26:6–13).

Our Lord comes first. If God occupies the central place in our Christian life, our dedication to others will be sincere. The Church's history is filled with the examples of saints who, because of their close union with God, gave up their material possessions to alleviate the needs of their neighbors. And we have many examples of this generosity today, including the religious sisters of St. Teresa of Calcutta, who dedicate many hours to Eucharistic adoration to draw strength to care for the poor and abandoned.

Service to God and service to neighbor

Service rendered to those in need, even when done without a religious motive, can and ordinarily does have a natural value and effectiveness. Nevertheless, this service only attains its proper Christian dimension and value when united to service to God, as its consequence

---

[18] St. Josemaría, *The Way*, no. 527.

and sign. Benedict XVI's commentary on Jesus' first temptation in the desert is very enlightening here.[19] Turning stones into bread would have meant exercising a merely worldly messianism restricted to resolving the material problems of society. Solving these problems is important humanly, but if done at the cost of service to God, the result is counter-productive:

> When this ordering of goods is no longer respected but turned on its head, the result is not justice or concern for human suffering. The result is rather ruin and destruction even of material goods themselves. When God is regarded as a secondary matter that can be set aside temporarily or permanently on account of more important things, it is precisely these supposedly more important things that come to nothing. It is not just the negative outcome of the Marxist experiment that proves this.[20]

It is God alone that we should adore and render worship to.

> Again, the devil took him to a very high mountain, and showed him all the kingdoms of the world and the glory of them, and he said to him, "All these I will give you, if you will fall down and worship me."

---

[19] See Joseph Ratzinger (Pope Benedict XVI), *Jesus of Nazareth: From the Baptism in the Jordan to the Transfiguration* (New York: Doubleday 2007), pp. 30–34.

[20] Ratzinger, *Jesus of Nazareth*, p. 33.

Then Jesus said to him, "Begone, Satan! for it is written, 'You shall worship the Lord your God and him only shall you serve.'" (Mt 4:8–10)

But the service and worship we render to God is not accepted by Him if we fail to love others. For as our Lord also said: "So if you are offering your gift at the altar, and there remember that your brother has something against you, leave your gift there before the altar and go, first be reconciled to your brother, and then come and offer your gift" (Mt 5:23–24). It is not sufficient, however, to be only reconciled with one's brother: in addition, *we should return and offer our gift at the altar.*

Part III

Loving Our Neighbor
and the World

Chapter 1

The Divine Precept

The Pharisee had just asked Jesus a question with the intention of trying to entrap him. After reminding this man that total and absolute love for God is the first and greatest of the commandments, Jesus added: "And a second is like it, You shall love your neighbor as yourself. On these two commandments depend all the law and the prophets" (Mt 22:39–40). The second commandment is like the first because it too commands us to love. But it is not the same, since our neighbor is not God, nor part of God. The love it prescribes is not the same as the love we owe to God; rather it is the same as the love we owe to ourselves.

Every other moral precept is an expression of these two: giving voice to either a requirement of love for God or love for neighbor. Hence the whole Christian law is characterized by love, not fear; and all the virtues receive from supernatural charity their "form" as a Christian virtue. Not even faith by itself would avail for salvation unless it were enlivened by charity. The Apostle James writes: "You believe that God is one; you do well. Even the demons believe—and shudder." (Jas 2:19).

And St. Paul insists: "Love is the fulfilling of the law" (Rom 13:10).

We have already mentioned that the precept of love for others was repeatedly set forth in the Old Testament. But Christ restored its authentic meaning, which little by little had become distorted by reducing "neighbor" to "relative," "friend," or "compatriot." "You have heard that it was said, 'You shall love your neighbor and hate your enemy.' But I say to you, Love your enemies and pray for those who persecute you" (Mt 5:43). As Pope Francis writes: "Fraternal love can only be gratuitous; it can never be a means of repaying others for what they have done or will do for us. That is why it is possible to love our enemies."[1] The freely-bestowed love that reaches out even to those who have harmed us is possible because we Christians are sustained by God's love: "We love, because he first loved us" (1 Jn 4:19). And this also bestows a great benefit on ourselves, since by forgiving others we become better children of God. Thus, after setting forth his teaching on love for our enemies, our Lord adds: "So that you may be sons of your Father who is in heaven" (Mt 5:45). Charity makes us resemble Jesus, the only-begotten Son of God, who from the cross intercedes for the very people who are taking his life (see Lk 23:23).

[1] Francis, *Laudato si*, no. 228.

The measure of charity

Moreover, as we have already mentioned, Christ has given a new and incomparably more sublime meaning to our love for neighbor, which reveals the true newness of Christian charity. "A new commandment I give to you, that you love one another; even as I have loved you" (Jn 13:34). Christ's love for us becomes the measure of our love for others. This is also a supernatural love, which God himself pours into our hearts. "May the God of steadfastness and encouragement grant you to live in such harmony with one another, in accord with Christ Jesus, that together you may with one voice glorify the God and Father of our Lord Jesus Christ. Welcome one another, therefore, as Christ has welcomed you for the glory of God" (Rom 15:5–7).

We are being asked to "love one another in the same way as Christ loves each one of us. Only then, by imitating the divine pattern he has left us, and notwithstanding our own rough ways, will we be able to open our hearts to all mankind and love in a higher and totally new way."[2] To love others as Christ loves us means welcoming and accompanying them as Christ has welcomed us. This entails more than simply putting up with their defects or with the bother they may cause us.

---

[2] St. Josemaría, *Friends of God*, no. 225.

Welcoming others means taking upon ourselves the responsibility, the burden, for the good of others, for their eternal happiness and their temporal happiness—just as Christ has welcomed and taken upon himself the whole burden of our sins to attain for us an eternal redemption.

The charity God asks of us is not restricted to the help we give our neighbor to meet a specific need. Rather it is a permanent attitude of constructive concern shown in deeds, which makes us be and feel responsible not only for what is our own, but also for everything that affects other men and women and the world. The commandment of love for God never leads to ignoring whatever is not God himself. On the contrary it spurs us, with a pressing and constant demand, to pour ourselves out in love for our neighbor, to take upon ourselves the burden of helping others to be happy, so as to truly live the law of Christ: "Bear one another's burdens, and so fulfill the law of Christ" (Gal 6:2).

The long tradition of Christian charitable activity testifies to this authentic concern for the welfare of each human being. In the first centuries of Christianity, we have the example of the deacon Lawrence's dedication to the poor, in whom, according to a Roman tradition, he saw the Church's real treasure. Nor has there been a shortage of institutes of religious life whose charism is to provide care for the most needy. Among other examples in recent history, we can cite the heroic dedication of St. Josemaría Escrivá to those suffering from contagious illnesses and the homeless in Madrid during the 1930's.[3]

Root and foundation of Christian love

The root and deepest source of Christian love for our neighbor, for our fellow men and women and the world, is precisely love for God. Let us listen once again to St. John in his First Letter:

> Beloved, let us love one another; for love is of God, and he who loves is born of God and knows God. He who does not love does not know God; for God is love. In this the love of God was made manifest among us, that God sent his only Son into the world, so that we might live through him. In this is love, not that we loved God but that he loved us and sent his Son to be the expiation for our sins. Beloved, if God so loved us, we also ought to love one another. (1 Jn 4:7–11)

Seeing every human being as the object of God's love leads us, if we truly love God, to love each and every person. "If any one says, 'I love God,' and hates his

---

[3] See Andrés Vazquez de Prada, *The Founder of Opus Dei*, vol. I (New York: Scepter Publishers, 2001), pp. 294–214, 323–329, and Julio Gonzalez Simancas Lacasa, *San Josemaría entre los enfermos de Madrid*, (1927–1931), "*Studia et Documenta*," vol II, no. 2, (2008), pp. 147–203. As of February 2017, available at http://multimedia.opusdei.org/pdf/es/san_josemar_eda_entre_los_enfermos.pdf.

brother, he is a liar; for he who does not love his brother whom he has seen, cannot love God whom he has not seen" (1 Jn 4:20). In commanding us to love himself, God also commands us to love others, as a necessary consequence: "And this commandment we have from him, that he who loves God should love his brother also" (1 Jn 4:21).

Every person is worthy of being loved

"Man . . . is the only creature on earth God willed for itself."[4] These words from the Second Vatican Ecumenical Council contain a wealth of meaning. God's love for the human person means that each human being possesses a radical dignity. A person may never be considered a mere means for some other end, because God loves that person for him or herself, not as a means for obtaining something else.

The second formulation of Kant's categorical imperative is: "Act in such a way that you treat humanity, whether in your own person or in the person of any other, never merely as a means to an end, but always at the same time as an end."[5] This imperative was meant to be

---

[4] Second Vatican Council, Pastoral Constitution on the Church in the Modern World *Gaudium et spes* (December 7, 1965), no. 24.

[5] Translated from Immanuel Kant, *Fundamentación de la metafísica de las costumbres* (Buenos Aires: Aguilar, 1973), pp. 111–112. For English see Imanual Kant, trans. Thomas Kingsmill Abbott, *Fundamental Principles of the Metaphysic of Morals*. As of February 2017, available at http://www.gutenberg.org/ebooks/5682.

a valid and definitive expression of the dignity of the human person. But in affirming the person as an end and never simply a means, Kant fails to offer sufficient grounding for the unity of the human person.[6]

By considering that God loves each person for him or herself, we can better grasp the natural basis of what we also know by faith: namely, that loving God is inseparably united with loving our neighbor as we do ourselves. Love for our neighbor is thus seen as a strictly human requirement, with a foundation far superior to the *simple omnis animal amat sibi simile* (every animal loves its like), which hardly proves sufficient for recognizing the precept of human fraternity as natural law. Loving our neighbor as we do ourselves means loving him for himself, not for ourselves, and thus loving him as God loves him. And we owe this love to everyone precisely in the measure that we ought to love God above everything else. As we said earlier, a total love for God requires, among other things, that we love everything that God loves, and for the same reason that he does.

Does this mean that all dependence or subordination of some people with respect to others is contrary to nature, to the human person's intrinsic dignity? Obviously not, since man is social by nature, and life in society

---

[6] See A. Rodriguez Luno, *Immanuel Kant: Fundamentación de la metafísica de las costumbres* Madrid: Magisterio Español, 1977), pp. 74–79. As of February 2017, available at https://www.scribd.com/document/243471523/KANT-Fundamentacion-Metafisica-de-las-Costumbres-1-pdf

necessarily entails the dependence of some of its members on others. We need only consider the family society, where the dependence of children on parents is clearly necessary; or society at large, which requires an effective authority and distinct functions, some subordinate to others. The "non-subordination" of the person, however, requires that the authority-obedience relationship be based on cooperation and mutual service, that is, on love; otherwise it is not worthy of the human person. Only in this way, moreover, can we understand that obedience not only is not contrary to freedom, but is an exercise of it.[7]

Beyond any "horizontal" humanism

Christian fraternity brings with it universal and permanent demands that no "horizontal" or merely earthly humanism can aspire to. We naturally, and almost by necessity, love other people who are united to us by ties of blood or friendship, and we do so with an affection that is not necessarily a consequence of love for God. Genuine and good in itself, such a love does not "contravene the sacred words,"[8] since it is in accord with human nature, a nature created by God. We can even love all mankind and the world with a genuine love that does not stem from love for God. Nevertheless, the moral integrity of this love, and its universal and permanent

[7] See St. Josemaría, *Friends of God*, nos. 23–38.
[8] St. Gregory the Great, *Homiliae in evangelia*, 27, I: PL 76, 1205 b.

standing, is far from secure. Let us not forget that genuine love cannot be grounded only on our neighbor's usefulness for us or what we get out of that person, since in that case we would be loving ourselves rather than our neighbor. This "love" would vanish as soon as that person's usefulness for our own well-being ceased.

Nevertheless, loving others in an upright manner is also the path for reaching love for God, just as we can reach knowledge of God by starting from our knowledge of the world. We can think here of the love good parents have for one another, which should be a common path for discovering God's love reflected in the husband's and wife's mutual affection.[9] Genuine human love can lead us to divine love, which in turn endows this human love with its deepest and fullest value.

> Human love, the love we experience on earth when it is really genuine, helps us to savor divine love. That is how we grasp the love by which we rejoice in God and which we will share in heaven when the Lord is "everything to everyone" (1 Cor 15:28). If we begin to understand God's love, we will feel impelled to become increasingly more compassionate, more generous, more dedicated.[10]

---

[9] See Guillame Derville, *Amor y desamor. La pureza liberadora* (Madrid: Rialp, 2015), pp. 157–158.

[10] St. Josemaría, *Christ Is Passing By*, no. 166.

Chapter 2

Requirements of Christian Fraternity

Our charity towards others ought to encompass, without any restrictions, all human beings and in a subordinate way, all creatures. The measure of this charity is the love Christ has for us—a love that went to the furthest possible extreme, "to the end" (Jn 13:1). It is impossible to have a greater love than our Lord's: "Greater love has no man than this, that a man lay down his life for his friends" (Jn 15:13). The question then arises: But is a universal love like this possible? Isn't it utopian? If we had to count exclusively on the strength of our own heart and will, on our natural capacity to love, then we would be wise to view this goal as illusory—despite the fact that the human will has the capacity to open itself to an ever-greater love, as we see in our own life and in that of others.

A Christian knows that this limitation is real and that love for all men and women is only truly attainable through the supernatural action of grace, which heals wounded human nature and elevates it. Supernatural charity is needed to love as Christ loves, which only God can grant. Hence on experiencing the limitation and even pettiness of our love, we need to raise a humble petition to heaven asking God to enlarge our heart. And then we can give thanks making use of those words of the Psalm: "*Dilatasti cor meum*—you enlarged my heart" (Ps 119:32). A Christian needs to be a person "capable of seeing the sacred grandeur of our neighbor, of finding God in every human being, of tolerating the nuisances of life in common by clinging to the love of God, of opening the heart to divine love and seeking the happiness of others just as their heavenly Father does."[1]

Only the sanctifying action of the Holy Spirit in our soul, identifying us with Christ, can make St. Paul's words a reality in our own life: "Have this mind among yourselves, which was in Christ Jesus" (Phil 5:2).

The order of charity

Since God asks us to love many different people (in reality, all men and women), our charity towards others needs to be *ordered*. The first requirement of this *order in charity* is subordinating all other loves to our love for God, which we have already spoken about above. Christ's words are very clear: "He who loves father or

[1] Pope Francis, Apostolic Exhortation on the Proclamation of the Gospel in Today's World *Evangelii gaudium* (November 24, 2013), no. 92.

mother more than me is not worthy of me; and he who loves son or daughter more than me is not worthy of me" (Mt 12:37).

However, putting God first in the order of charity must be correctly understood. The love we owe God is not *the first in a series*, which the concept of order could seem to suggest. Rather, it is a love that should not only be *greater* but also *qualitatively distinct* from all other loves. That is, it should be an absolute love, and encompass all other loves, including our love for others. This subordination to God does not diminish the quality of our love for neighbor, but rather incomparably elevates it. It leads to loving others as God loves them, though we will never be able to equal the love God has for each and every human being. Hence an apparent love for others that separates us from God's love is never a true love.

While love for others is a necessary sign of our love for God, love for God will also be a sign that our love for others is truly Christian. For as St. John says succinctly: "By this we know that we love the children of God, when we love God and obey his commandments" (1 Jn 5:2).

The order of charity stems, also in the natural order, from the similarity between the lover and the loved one: "*similitudo est causa dilectionis*—likeness causes love."[2]

---

[2] St. Thomas, *Summa theologiae*, II-II, q. 26, a. 2 ad 2.

Therefore, a greater love is owed by nature (human nature itself inclines us to this) to those who are more like us. In first place, a likeness of nature, and so we should love, above all other creatures, our fellow human beings. And, among these, we should love first those who are united to us by spiritual, family, or social ties. But it is not a matter of establishing a rigid order among the different objects of our love, which is not an easy task and may even be counterproductive. Nor, paradoxically, does loving some people more than others (required by the order of charity) mean *loving others less*. Rather it means loving them first, carrying out deeds of love first with some specific people and not others.

The fact that we are more like other human beings than we are like God might lead us to think we should love them more than God, or before Him. However, as St. Thomas Aquinas explains: "The likeness we have to God precedes and causes the likeness we have to our neighbor: because from the very fact that we share along with our neighbor in something received from God, we become like to our neighbor. Hence by reason of this likeness we ought to love God more than we love our neighbor."[3] And also: "God is loved as the cause of happiness, whereas our neighbor is loved as receiving together with us a share of happiness from Him."[4]

---

[3] St. Thomas, *Summa theologiae*, II-II, q. 26, a. 2 ad 2.
[4] St. Thomas, *Summa theologiae*, II-II, q. 26, a. 2 c.

Charity and unity in the faith

Another important aspect of the order of charity is set forth by St. Paul in his Letter to the Galatians: "So then, as we have opportunity, let us do good to all men, and especially to those who are of the household of faith" (6:10). We have to love our brothers and sisters in the faith *before* the rest of humanity. This primacy of our love for those possessing the same faith is not only, or mainly, a "tactical" one of maintaining the unity essential to the development of the Church, the community of believers. Rather the underlying reason is found in the similarity that love presupposes. Supernatural life entails an interior, ontological reality: divine filiation, grace that elevates human nature, virtues that raise our human faculties to the supernatural order. This elevation results in a profound newness in the human person, which entails a primacy of love towards those, who like us, share in this gift of grace, a participation in the divine nature (see 2 Pt 1:4).

Moreover, although we should always strive to love also non-Catholics and even declared enemies of the Church, this love would not be ordered if it coexisted with a certain aversion or lack of understanding for our brothers and sisters in the faith who, in matters open to personal opinion, held a different position than our own. It would be a shame to find that this Italian saying could sometimes be applied to Catholics: "*amico dei nemici e nemico degli amici*—a friend of the enemies and an enemy of the friends."

Learning to love, by contemplating Jesus Christ

To learn to love, we must contemplate Jesus, because his love for us, as we have already said, is the measure and paradigm of Christian charity.

> If we don't learn from Jesus, we will never love. If, like some people, we were to think that to keep a clean heart, a heart worthy of God, means "not mixing it up, not contaminating it" with human affection, we would become insensitive to other people's pain and sorrow. We would be capable only of an "official charity," something dry and soulless. But ours would not be the true charity of Jesus Christ, which involves affection and human warmth."[5]

The supernatural is not juxtaposed to the natural as though added to it externally, for grace presupposes, heals, and elevates nature; it does not replace it. Thus, supernatural charity for others presupposes natural human love, in order to heal it and raise it up. And like human love, it involves not only our will but also our feelings. As in everything, we have Christ's example to guide us:

How wonderful it is for God to love with a man's

---

[5] St. Josemaría, *Christ Is Passing By*, no. 167.

heart. . . . The Gospels tell us that Jesus had no place to rest his head, but they also tell us that he had many good, close friends, eager to have him stay in their homes when he was in the vicinity. They tell us of his compassion for the sick, of his sorrow for those who were ignorant or in error, his anger at the money changers who profaned the temple; his heart was touched by the sorrow of the widow at Naim.[6]

Just as our love for God is not only a sentiment, but also leads to deeds manifesting that love, so our love for others should also be a love shown with deeds. St. John tells us in his First Letter, which is as it were a "magna carta" of Christian charity: "Let us not love in word or speech but in deed and in truth" (3:18). "Works of love directed to our neighbor are the most perfect external manifestation of the interior grace of the Spirit."[7]

Love for others and apostolate

Works of love, deeds of service to our neighbor, also have a clear order. Since love leads to wanting and seeking the good of the person loved, the order of charity leads to wanting and seeking principally the union of others with God, since this is the greatest good, the definitive one, outside of which no other partial good has

[6] St. Josemaría, *Christ Is Passing By*, no. 108.
[7] Francis, *Evangelii gaudium*, no. 37.

full meaning. Seeking the spiritual good of others is apostolate, a mission our Lord entrusted to the Apostles and, through them, to all Christians, to each in accord with his or her specific circumstances: "Go into all the world and preach the gospel to the whole creation" (Mk 16:15). The Church's entire mission can be summed up in this "*traditio Evangelii*," transmitting the Gospel to all mankind. Here "the Gospel" should be understood in its Pauline sense, as "the power of God for salvation to everyone who has faith" (Rom 1:16), made present principally in the Word and the sacraments.

Apostolate, evangelization in all its forms, must be carried out by the witness of one's life as well as with words. It is a mission entrusted to everyone, not only to priests. All the baptized receive from our Lord this mission, which they must carry out with a deep ecclesial sense, without any need for a mandate from the Church's hierarchy. In particular, there is a great need for apostolate on the part of the laity, carried out amidst all earthly realities: "The layman's specific role in the mission of the Church is precisely that of sanctifying secular reality, the temporal order, the world, *ab intra*, in an immediate and direct way."[8]

In the midst of their ordinary life, with its varied family, professional, and social relationships, lay people can unite in many different ways the witness of their life and

---

[8] St. Josemaría, *Conversations with St. Josemaría Escrivá*, no. 9; see Vatican II, Lumen gentium, no. 35.

their words announcing the Gospel. Thus, each in accord with his or her possibilities can contribute to imbuing with Christ's spirit professional and social institutions, the mass media, etc. Especially important is the person-to-person transmission of the Gospel, within a dialogue of sincere friendship, by which lay people "exercise their apostolate in the world like leaven."[9]

Also, because it accords with an important anthropological reality, this personal transmission of the Gospel has a special effectiveness: the interpersonal dialogue by which one who has received a good seeks to communicate it to others. Apostolic dialogue comes about naturally when there is sincere friendship. This is not a matter of "instrumentalizing" friendship, but rather of helping friends to share in the great good of the faith and friendship with Christ. As Benedict XVI said in the homily for the solemn inauguration of his pontificate: "There is nothing more beautiful than to be surprised by the Gospel, by the encounter with Christ. There is nothing more beautiful than to know Him and to speak to others of our friendship with Him."[10]

In contrast, seeking for oneself or for others only material goods would be a form of paganism: "Do not be

---

[9] Vatican II, Decree on the Apostolate of the Laity *Apostolicam actuositatem* (November 18, 1965), no. 2. As of February 2017 available at http://www.vatican.va/archive/hist_councils/ii_vatican_council/documents/vat-ii_decree_19651118_apostolicam-actuositatem_en.html.

[10] Pope Benedict XVI, Homily, April 24, 2005. As of February 2017, available at https://w2.vatican.va/content/benedict-xvi/en/homilies/2005/documents/hf_ben-xvi_hom_20050424_inizio-pontificato.html.

anxious, saying 'What shall we eat?' or 'What shall we drink?' or 'What shall we wear?' For the Gentiles seek all these things, and your heavenly Father knows that you need them all. But seek first his kingdom and his righteousness, and all these things shall be yours as well" (Mt 6:32–33).[11]

If our love for others and the world is to be like Christ's love, we should not forget that our Lord was not concerned, in the first place, with freeing people from social and economic oppression (no less present twenty centuries ago than it is today). Certainly, Christ was moved by people's misery and suffering, and he asks us to strive to eliminate them. But above all—because his love was and is the greatest love possible—he suffers on seeing people's ignorance and sin. His mission on earth was precisely to redeem us from sin, a true, radical slavery, principally through the Sacrifice of the Cross: "Be imitators of God, as beloved children. And walk in love, as Christ loved us and gave himself up for us, a fragrant offering and sacrifice to God" (Eph 5:1–2).

The primacy of spiritual good over all material good is a requirement of the order in Christian charity. But it should never be taken as an excuse for disregarding the material well-being of others, since charity also embraces this concern.

---

[11] See Vatican Council II, *Gaudium et spes*, no. 72

A man or a society that does not react to suffering and injustice and makes no effort to alleviate them is still distant from the love of Christ's heart. While Christians enjoy the fullest freedom in finding and applying various solutions to these problems, they should be united in having one and the same desire to serve mankind. Otherwise their Christianity will not be the word and life of Jesus; it will be a fraud, a deception of God and man.[12]

The Church has always insisted on the importance of this dimension of charity, which Holy Scripture expresses with divine eloquence. When Tobias prepares to leave on a long journey, he receives from his father some advice that is, as it were, a summary of the Law:

Remember the Lord our God all your days, my son, and refuse to sin or to transgress his commandments. Love uprightly all the days of your life, and do not walk in the ways of wrong doing. . . . Give alms from your possessions to all who live uprightly, and do not let your eye begrudge the gift when you make it. Do not turn your face away from any poor man, and the face of God will not be turned away from you. If you have many possessions, make your gift from them in proportion; if few, do not be afraid

<hr />

[12] St. Josemaría, *Christ Is Passing By*, no. 167.

to give according to the little you have. . . . Do not hold over till the next day the wages for any man who works for you. . . . Give of your bread to the hungry, and of your clothing to the naked. . . . Bless the Lord God on every occasion; ask him that your ways may be made straight and that all your paths and plans may prosper. . . . So, my son, remember my commands, and do not let them be blotted out of your mind. (Tb 4:5–19)

Charity and justice

A stringent requirement of charity towards our neighbor is the need for justice. Without justice, our charity would be a false charity. Nor can we settle for a justice without charity, because even though it has value in itself, it is not the justice that God's justice (his holiness) asks of us.

Charity presupposes and vivifies justice. The charity we show in attending to the material needs of others is so important that Christ, when speaking about the final judgment, declared:

When the Son of man comes in his glory and all the angels with him, then he will sit on his glorious throne. Before him will be gathered all the nations and he will separate them one from another as a shepherd separates the sheep from the goats, and he will place the sheep at his right hand, but the goats at the left. Then the King will say to those at his right hand, "Come, O blessed of my Father, inherit the kingdom prepared for you from the foundation of the world, for I was hungry and you gave me food, I was thirsty and you gave me drink, I was a stranger and you welcomed me, I was naked and you clothed me, I was sick and you visited me, I was in prison and you came to me." Then the righteous will answer him, "Lord, when did we see you hungry and feed you, or thirsty and give you drink? And when did we see you a stranger and welcome you, or naked and clothe you? And when did we see you sick or in prison and visit you?" And the King will answer them, "Truly, I say to you, as you did it to one of the least of these my brethren, you did it to me" (Mt 25:31–40).

And Jesus goes on to warn those who failed to do so of the danger of eternal condemnation (see Mt 25:41–46).

Regarding this parable, Benedict XVI wrote:

We should especially mention the great parable of the Last Judgement (cf. Mt 25:31–46), in which love becomes the criterion for the definitive decision about a human life's worth or lack thereof. Jesus identifies himself with those in need, with the hungry, the thirsty, the stranger, the naked, the sick and those in prison. "As you did it to one of the least of these my brethren, you did it to me" (Mt 25:40). Love of God and love of neighbor have become one: in the least of the brethren we find Jesus himself, and in Jesus we find God.[13]

However, we should never forget that all these external works would be worthless for attaining eternal life if we were to lack *charity*,[14] if love for God and love for others, with human and supernatural affection, were lacking. This is not simply a matter of carrying out *works of charity*, for this virtue is not restricted to giving alms or other similar gestures. Charity is not something we *do*, but something we *have*; and then it overflows in deeds of service. And "charity consists not so much in giving as in understanding."[15] Without understanding, there is no love; and if love is lacking, there is no true Christian charity.

Mankind's deepest hope

To be understanding, we need to rejoice with those who rejoice and suffer with those who suffer, for "*ex amore procedit et gaudium et tristitia*—joy and sorrow stem from love."[16] This entails doing all we can to prevent people from suffering and to foster and increase their joy. Understanding is needed to realize that the true and prin-

[13] Benedict XVI, *Deus caritas est*, no. 15.
[14] See the words from 1 Cor 13:1–3 quoted above.
[15] St. Josemaría, *The Way*, no. 463.
[16] St. Thomas, *Summa Theologiae*, II-II, q. 28, a. 1.

cipal good of others lies in their union with God. This is the source of authentic and enduring joy here on earth, and leads to the complete happiness found only in heaven. This truth—in no sense a facile consolation for the poor, for those who suffer—is mankind's deepest hope, giving us the realization that we are God's children and co-heirs with Christ to eternal life. Therefore, Christians should have a profound dominion over all the realities of this world, bestowing only relative importance on them. Only God is absolute. And with St. Paul we can say: "For I am sure that that neither death, nor life, nor angels, nor principalities, nor things present, nor things to come, nor powers, nor height, nor depth, nor anything else in all creation, will be able to separate us from the love of God in Christ Jesus our Lord" (Rom 8:38–39).

To rob people of this hope by replacing it with the hope of a purely earthly and material happiness would be fraudulent. Sooner or later, on realizing how precarious and even utopian this hope is, it can lead only to the darkest despair. So, Pope Francis warns us: "Please do not let yourselves be robbed of hope!"[17]

Christian service to our neighbor demands a great deal of us. Both our will and our feelings need to be engaged in this effort, leading to many specific deeds.

[17] Pope Francis, *Homily*, March 24, 2013. As of February 2017, available at http://w2.vatican.va/content/francesco/en/homilies/2013/documents/papa-francesco_20130324_palme.html.

Faced with this great challenge, with the help of God's grace, Christians won't cower or become flustered and nervous. But neither can they remain tranquil, because "*caritas Christi urget nos*—the love of Christ impels us" (2 Cor 5:14).

> In the name of this victorious love of Christ, we Christians should go out into the world to be sowers of peace and joy through everything we say and do. We have to fight—a fight of peace—against evil, against injustice, against sin. Thus do we serve notice that the present condition of mankind is not definitive. Only the love of God, shown in the heart of Christ, will attain the glorious spiritual triumph of men.[18]

Sowing peace and joy

Christians must be sowers of peace and joy in the world, which means bringing peace and joy to people's hearts and to society. All the books of the New Testament (except the First Letter of St. John) give a prominent place to peace, seen above all as a gift from Christ that the world cannot give: "Peace I leave with you; my peace I give to you; not as the world gives do I give to you" (Jn 14:27). We can view this peace as Christ himself, who gives himself to us: "*Ipse est enim pax nostra*—for he is our peace" (Eph 2:14). Jesus has reconciled us with the Fa-

[18] St. Josemaría, *Christ Is Passing By*, no. 168.

ther (see Rom 5:10) and united us with himself and
with one another, as brothers and sisters.

The literal meaning of these words from the second
chapter of Ephesians, as the immediate context makes
clear, is the peace between the Jews and Christians that
Christ achieved by breaking down the wall of separation
between them. But in a broader context, the breaking
down of the wall of separation refers to the insertion of
the Jews and Gentiles into one single body, the Body of
Christ. Hence on one hand, peace is joined to recon-
ciliation with God, to justification (see Rom 5:10), and
therefore to the grace of filial adoption. On the other
hand, whoever is united to Christ, our peace, should
break down walls of separation and be a peacemaker, a
characteristic proper to the children of God: "Blessed
are the peacemakers, for they shall be called sons of
God" (Mt 5:9). In our world, with no lack of tensions
and divisions created by men, Christians are called to
overcome barriers and strive to foster the "culture of
encounter" that begins with a personal encounter with
Christ.[19]

Peace must be authentic, and not the fruit of a false
"irenicism" that, in the name of peace and concord,
seeks to place divine truth and human error on the

[19] See Francis, *Address*, March 29, 2014. As of February 2017, available at
https://w2.vatican.va/content/francesco/en/speeches/2014/march/
documents/papa-francesco_20140329_movimento-ciechi-missione-sor-
domuti.html.

same level, fleeing from the persecution and discord that Christ foretold for those who are faithful to him: "Blessed are those who are persecuted for righteousness' sake, for theirs is the kingdom of heaven. Blessed are you when men revile you and persecute you and utter all kinds of evil against you falsely on my account. Rejoice and be glad, for your reward is great in heaven" (Mt 5:10–12).

Loving and serving the world has to be for us the necessary consequence of our loving and serving God. But we must do so with a disinterested love, without seeking applause or earthly compensations. And with great fortitude since: "If the world hates you, know that it has hated me before it hated you. If you were of the world, the world would love its own; but because you are not of the world, but I chose you out of the world, therefore the world hates you. Remember the word that I said to you, 'A servant is not greater than his master'" (Jn 15:18–20).

Epilogue

Perhaps it was more frequent some years ago than now to encounter people who viewed modern times as a period marking the end of the "conventional Christianity" that had prevailed since the peace of Constantine, making way for a new Christianity that would in essence be a compromise with the world, thanks to a new appreciation of the Gospel's missionary spirit.

Underlying this attitude was an unfounded prejudice (which may still be present in some sectors): thinking that essential aspects of the Christian message had become adulterated or obscured over centuries in the life of the Church. This hasty and unjust judgment diverges from the faith itself of the Church, since it is impossible that the Holy Spirit, who guides the People of God, the Body of Christ, could have allowed such a universal and long-lasting error to occur. The supreme Magisterium of the Church confirmed this faith in God and in the Church centuries ago when it condemned as heretical the proposition: "in recent centuries there has been a widespread obscuring of truths of the gravest importance to religion, which are the foundation of Christ's moral teaching."[1]

---

[1] Pius VI, Apostolic Constitution *Auctorem fidei*, August 28, 1794: DS 2601.

The faith that has been lived in the Church for twenty centuries is not open to substantial change. However, there is certainly room for constant progress in better understanding the immense wealth contained in the Gospel, and above all for greater personal faithfulness to Christ. But not for any novelty in this Gospel: "But even if we, or an angel from heaven, should preach a gospel contrary to that which we preached to you, let him be accursed. As we have said before, so now I say again, If anyone is preaching to you a gospel contrary to that which you received, let him be accursed" (Gal 1:8–9).

The serious and challenging demands of Christian charity have always been the same. Every epoch in human history has witnessed both heroism and cowardice, sanctity and sin. To live as Christ asks us, there is no need to invent another Christianity. Rather we need to be personally more faithful to our Lord. Christian *aggiornamento*, today as always, means being faithful.[2] Blessed Paul VI reminded us: "No one may desire novelty in the Church where novelty would mean betrayal of the norm of faith; faith is not invented, nor manipulated: It is received, guarded and lived."[3]

If we truly want to serve mankind and the world, and thereby fulfill our Lord's command, we must love God first. For only in this love and through this love will our service to others—love shown in deeds—be able to imi-

[2] See St. Josemaría, *Conversations with St. Josemaría Escrivá*, no. 1.
[3] Blessed Paul VI, *Audience*, August 4, 1971.

tate the incomparable grandeur of Christ's heart. In
contrast, Christ's words and human history always re-
mind us that setting aside God and the hope for eternity
never lead to greater love and service to mankind and
the world.

> Come, Lord Jesus! This is the cry of the Church that
> rings out in the last verse of the Apocalypse and that
> is heard throughout the world's entire history. We
> men, unfortunately, are quite quick to forget eternal
> perspectives and to seek a definitive home here be-
> low. And thus, if this prompt coming of Christ is no
> longer looked for, the danger exists of first begin-
> ning to hope that it will be delayed, and eventually
> to hope that it will never take place. This abdication
> of Christian hope would spell the death of Christian-
> ity and the irremediable decadence of the Church.
> Then we would witness, according to our Lord's par-
> able, that scene of the servants carousing and beat-
> ing one another (Mt 24:33 ff.), telling themselves:
> "The master is delayed, he is not coming."
>
> Servants like these, without faith or hope, will al-
> ways be found. But there will also always be faithful
> servants who, with loins girded and lamps lit, watch
> during the long night without growing weary for
> their master's return: "Come, Lord Jesus!"[4]

---

[4] Translated from Julio Lebreton, *La vida y doctrina de Jesucristo Nuestro Señor* (Madrid: Editorial Razon y Fe, 1959), pp. 431–432.